UNIVERSITY OF NOTTINGHAM

10 0230773 X

WITHDRAWN

FROM THE LIBRARY

WITH GOD, FOR
THE PEOPLE

D0533050

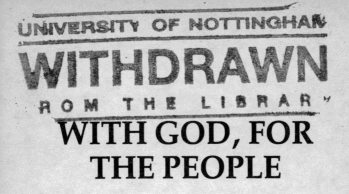
UNIVERSITY OF NOTTINGHAM
WITHDRAWN
ROM THE LIBRARY

WITH GOD, FOR THE PEOPLE

The autobiography of
Laszlo Tokes

**as told to
David Porter**

UNIVERSITY LIBRARY
NOTTINGHAM

HODDER & STOUGHTON
LONDON SYDNEY AUCKLAND TORONTO

100230T3X

British Library Cataloguing in Publication Data

Tokes, Laszlo
  With God, for the people: the autobiography
  of Laszlo Tokes.
  1. Romania. Tokes, Laszlo.
  I. Title   II. Porter, David, *1945–*
  949.803

  ISBN 0-340-54152-0

*Copyright © Laszlo Tokes and David Porter. First published in Great Britain
1990. All rights reserved. No part of this publication may be reproduced or
transmitted in any form or by any means, electronic or mechanical, including
photocopying, recording, or any information storage or retrieval system,
without either prior permission in writing from the publisher or a licence
permitting restricted copying. In the United Kingdom such licences are issued
by the Copyright Licensing Agency, 33–34 Alfred Place, London WC1E 7DP.
The right of Laszlo Tokes and David Porter to be identified as the authors of this
work has been asserted by them in accordance with the Copyright, Designs and
Patents Act 1988. Published by Hodder and Stoughton, a division of Hodder
and Stoughton Ltd, Mill Road, Dunton Green, Sevenoaks, Kent TN13 2YA.
Editorial Office: 47 Bedford Square, London WC1B 3DP. Photoset by Rowland
Phototypesetting Ltd, Bury St Edmunds, Suffolk. Printed in Great Britain by
Cox and Wyman Ltd, Reading, Berks.*

Acknowledgments

This book is the autobiography of Laszlo Tokes. It is told by him from his own viewpoint. Others will no doubt write books about the Romanian Revolution and Laszlo Tokes's role in it, but this is his own story, carefully told over many hours spread over many weeks.

However, in working with Laszlo Tokes on his book, I have received help, encouragement and friendship from many people.

My debt is greatest to Laszlo Tokes himself. This book was written during the first half of 1990 when the demands upon him were many and heavy. His many hours of conversation with me were taken from time that would otherwise have been used for much needed recreation, and relaxation with his family. He also arranged for me to have access to his personal records and correspondence. I am also grateful to Edit Tokes and Mrs Erzsebet Tokes, who not only tolerated my arriving with Laszlo Tokes on several of his necessarily rare visits home, but welcomed me warmly and gave me hospitality. Laszlo's father, Istvan, kindly supplied information by telephone.

In Oradea, I was given hospitality and much information by Attila Veres-Kovacs, Deputy Bishop of Oradea, and his wife. The bishop's secretary, Rev Sandor Fazakas, also provided help. Many members of the Oradea diocese clergy welcomed me in their parishes.

Out of a long list of people, I am particularly grateful to the congregation of Timisoara Hungarian Reformed Church, and most especially to Lajos Varga and his family, who gave me information and documentation, showed me round the city and provided generous hospitality, usually at a moment's notice. Jozsef Kabai and his family also gave me warm hospitality, and Arpad Gazda contributed invaluable recollections of his own arrest on December 16th. The Varga family in Mineu allowed me to interview them and showed me round the village. I am grateful, too, to Professor Tamas Juhasz of Cluj Theological Institute for hospitality and a most helpful interview. The staff of the Reformed Diocese of Debrecen, Hungary, have given me help and encouragement.

Four Hungarians in particular have made this book possible. Dora Bernhardt of Budapest, who invited me to Hungary for the first time in the dying days of the Eastern bloc, has been an invaluable friend and adviser. Balint Bessenyey, also of Budapest, has been overwhelmingly generous in his hospitality and informative in his discussions about the book. Dezso Abraham welcomed me on a number of occasions with graciousness and generosity.

Most of all, Istvan and Csilla Geczy of Letavertes have given me hospitality and help that I value enormously. Istvan has driven me thousands of miles in Romania and Hungary while writing this book and contributed to it in countless ways. Through sharing in the writing of this book, we have become friends.

Finally, the BBC World Service (Hungarian Department) and the Hungarian Reformed Church in London have both given assistance, and a number of Christian organisations operating in Eastern Europe have provided research facilities and other help. Catharine Brown of Liss has provided translation help.

Christoph and Lili Steurer of Vienna have taken a supportive and creative interest in this book from its very beginning; it was Christoph who first suggested I should write about Eastern Europe. His brother-in-law, Siegfried Molnar, gave me great assistance with transport and interpretation.

A major contribution to the book is the many hours that my wife, Tricia, spent in transcribing tapes of interviews. A professional photographer, she also processed the photographs I brought back from Romania and the technical quality of the prints reflects her professional expertise. In addition, my whole family has supported me in many ways during several lengthy absences in Eastern Europe.

DAVID PORTER

Contents

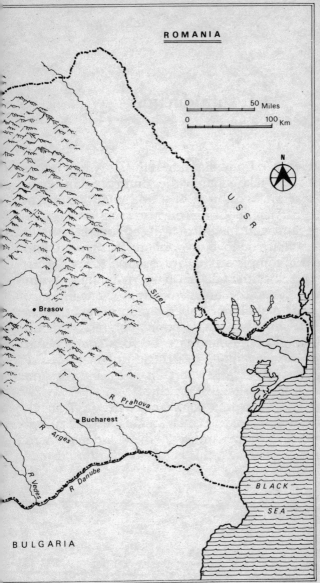

ROMANIA

0   50 Miles
0   100 Km

N

U S S R

R Siret

• Brasov

R Prahova

R Arges

• Bucharest

R Danube

R Vedea

BLACK

SEA

BULGARIA

Introduction

If you want to understand best the story that is told in this book, take a map of the country in which you live; tear off two-thirds of it and give those two-thirds to a neighbouring country.

The land you have lost will, of course, contain country that you love, major natural resources and industrial complexes that are essential to your economy and cities and villages in which millions of your countrymen and countrywomen live. Imagine also that your neighbour embarks on a programme of forced assimilation, mass population resettlement, prohibition of the language of your country and finally the systematic destruction of most of the villages and a large part of the cultural and architectural heritage of the cities.

The events in this book took place in Transylvania, now part of Romania, and historically part of Hungary. No other country in the world in modern times has lost two-thirds of its territory to its neighbours.

A Note on Language

It was a policy of the Ceausescu regime to demand that Hungarian place names be abandoned and that their Romanian equivalents be used.

The Hungarian community in Romania, when talking of towns that were built by Hungarians and were Hungarian within the living memory of some, often use the Hungarian names, not merely out of sentiment but to make a point about their diminishing cultural heritage and the forced Romanianisation of many of their communities.

Ideally, as a Hungarian Romanian, I would like to use Hungarian place names, as my parents taught me. In everyday conversation I use both, but in telling my story I would prefer to use Hungarian. The right to use Hungarian names was denied us by Ceausescu and was won back at the cost of many lives.

However, the practical problem is that no maps are available using Hungarian place names and readers wishing to follow the story on a map would have great difficulty in identifying the places mentioned.

As a compromise I have used the Hungarian version for the three Transylvanian cities that play the largest part in this book and for most other places I have used the Romanian.

Readers should note therefore that in the West, Temesvar is usually called Timisoara, Kolozsvar is called Cluj or Cluj-Napoca, and Nagyvarad is called Oradea.

1

TEMESVAR – DECEMBER 15TH

The Securitate thugs had smashed every window in my apartment weeks ago. In my study, the broken panes were boarded and shuttered against the early morning light. If I were to fling them open and look out I would see the windows of the building across the street; anonymous apertures in the formal city block, with drab net curtains hiding the interior of the rooms. Those windows had the same excellent view of mine across the quiet leafy side street. From behind the dirty curtains, Ceausescu's hated secret police had been watching me and my family for several months. At my front door, I knew, the regular Securitate guard was stationed, recording every activity and every visitor.

I looked around my study. A comfortable room; not grand, but crowded with familiar things, the characteristic possessions of a Hungarian Transylvanian family. Some original paintings hung on the walls and there were rows of ornamental plates from various villages. The bookshelves were full: volumes of the poetry I had loved since my childhood; several of my father's theological writings, annotated by myself in neat, careful handwriting; other theological tomes that I had struggled to master as a theological student. In the corner, the enormous Hungarian wood stove burned fitfully. Though it was midwinter, we had very little firewood. The Securitate had seen to that. The chill from the biting winter morning outside struck through the boarded windows.

My desk was unusually tidy. Everything was arranged in precise order. I kept few confidential papers in my study now, especially since the Securitate's break-in a few weeks ago. But usually the desk of a working pastor is full of half-finished business, sermons in preparation, church papers and the like. There was none of that to be seen on mine. I had sorted out my affairs and made my arrangements. It was December 15th, 1989: the day I was to be forcibly removed from my home and dismissed as pastor of the Hungarian Reformed Church, Temesvar.

It was nine o'clock in the morning. My wife Edit and I were alone in the apartment. Our small son Mate was in Kolozsvar, staying with his grandparents. Edit was pregnant with our second child.

I read again the brief note I had received in August from Laszlo Papp, Bishop of Nagyvarad. He and I had been locked in confrontation for years. My offence: complaining about a shortage of hymnbooks; organising youth activities in the church; protesting against the destruction of the Romanian villages; appearing on a foreign television programme and speaking against the brutal oppression of Ceausescu's regime.

The terse half-sheet of paper bearing the rubber stamp of the bishop's office in Nagyvarad stated

that I would have to vacate my apartment by
December 15th. As from August 20th I was no
longer pastor in Temesvar; another minister would
be sent to replace me. I was to be transferred to the
parish of Mineu, an isolated mountain village.
Pinned to the letter was a later one dated the beginning of December. It was a notice of eviction. My
appeal against the bishop's earlier ruling had failed.
I would have to leave, or be removed by force, in
eight days' time.

The previous Sunday I had stood in the pulpit and
addressed a congregation that filled the pews and
the balcony. Many of the people had regularly
smuggled firewood and food into the church for us,
defying the orders of the Securitate who stood
guard outside the building noting all who entered.
It was the same every Sunday. In the church that
morning were people who had risked their lives for
my wife and myself. And I knew that sitting among
the congregation, bored by the service but listening
to every word I said, were plain-clothes Securitate
officers.

I'd made my announcement with a heavy heart.
'Dear brothers and sisters in Christ, I have been
issued with a summons of eviction. I will not accept
it, so I will be taken from you by force next Friday.'
The sober faces betrayed no surprise. It was the
inevitable outcome of long months of self-imposed
imprisonment in my own home, months in which
mounting pressure from the church authorities,
police and Securitate had pointed to this inevitable
outcome. 'It is an illegal act,' I explained; and so it
was, for the pastor's apartment, like church pre-
mises in most countries, was considered the
possession of the local church and its members.

'They want to do this in secret because they have no right to do it.'

The congregation listened in silence. Some of the people sitting there would report my words to their Securitate superiors as soon as the service was over. 'Please, come next Friday and be witnesses of what will happen. Come, be peaceful, but be witnesses.'

As the people filed out I had wondered how many of them would turn up next Friday. Very few, I guessed. Nor did I expect, or want, them to resist my eviction. Morally, I had no right to demand that. There had been so much persecution against them and they were in so much fear that I doubted they had courage left to stand against this last phase. And I was responsible for these men and women. They were my flock and I was their pastor. I just wanted them to be there, to observe what was going to happen, so that nobody would ever be able to persuade them that things had been done differently.

I went to the window and pulled one of the boards aside to ventilate the room. The cold air rushed at my face and I blinked in the bright sunlight. Despite the cutting chill, it was a beautiful, almost spring-like morning. Gradually, my eyes adjusted to the light.

Several dozen members of my congregation were standing in small groups on the pavement outside. As I leaned further out to look past the corner of the building I could see others standing in the main road. There were thirty or forty people, at least.

Lajos Varga, church member and friend of Laszlo Tokes: *One of the chief characteristics of Laszlo Tokes is that he keeps nothing from us. All of us in the church knew that the Securitate had been threatening him and his*

*family – the surveillance, the intimidation, the violence.
So when he told us that he was going to be arrested on
Friday and asked us to come – not to bring sticks and
stones, just to be observers – we came.*

*Of course we were very frightened. We stood in small
groups of three or four, some in the side street, some in the
main street, and we waited. Nobody knew quite what to
expect. 'Has anything happened yet? What's going on?
Have the Securitate done anything yet?'*

*Then Laszlo appeared at the window and made a sign
with his arm for us to come forward. Though we did not
know it then, it was the beginning of the Revolution. At
last something was happening. The Securitate guards
could just be seen in the entrance. They were watching the
crowd.*

*About thirty of us moved to the window. Many old men
and women who had not yet gone to work were among us.
We called up to Laszlo Tokes, 'What can we do to help?
Have they tried to evict you? What do you want us to do?'*

I looked down at the people. If I had asked them to
pick up stones and attack the Securitate they would
probably have done it. I wanted them to stay, but I
didn't want to bring them into danger.

'Nobody has tried to evict us,' I assured them.
'We are safe. Thank you for coming. But perhaps
you should go home now.' It was a half-hearted
suggestion, rejected immediately by the crowd. I
wondered how to occupy them, to avoid the situation getting out of hand. Though some were
drifting away to go to work, others were arriving.

Suddenly I remembered the empty cupboards in
the kitchen.

'We have no food,' I told them. 'No bread, no
milk. If you could please . . .'

'Immediately!' several voices responded, and a number of people disappeared in search of food. A subtle change had come over the people; now they had something to do. They weren't just passive spectators any more.

Soon food was brought to the window. By now the numbers around the window had doubled. A tall man was found to hand it up to me. I took it to Edit, and we ate some breakfast. From time to time I went back to the open window and spoke to the people outside.

Temesvar Hungarian Reformed Church is in an apartment block near the Bega Canal; the pastor's apartment is on the first floor, the church hall itself on the second. The front door of our apartment opened on to a half-landing, from which stone steps descended to the main entrance in the side street. Church members were now thronging that entrance, where the Securitate guards were standing. At both ends of the street Securitate cars had now been parked, and officers were standing nearby mingling with the crowd. For the present the situation was a stalemate.

So far as the authorities knew, I might be planning to leave peacefully later in the day; no attempt was made to force an entry into the church building. Any direct action might provoke a reaction from the crowd. There had been a minor demonstration over food shortages in Brasov only days ago; the Securitate would prefer not to have the same happen here. So both sides sat and waited.

At ten, we heard angry voices shouting in the main entrance. We peered out of our front door. A man and a woman were arguing with two men in military uniform whom we had not seen before. They were demanding to be allowed to visit us. By their voices we knew they were Americans.

'They are all right. We are protecting them,' insisted the militia.

'They're lying,' we shouted down the steps. 'Make them let you pass.'

The soldiers turned on us. 'Be quiet!' they demanded. 'Go back into your apartment.'

'It is *my* apartment,' I retorted firmly, 'and you cannot give orders in my home.' The militia became extremely angry. The visitors could have been in no doubt that they were lying, that we were under forced surveillance. After a few minutes the soldiers pushed the visitors out. 'If you want to come here you will have get permission from the town hall,' they said. We knew such permission would never be granted.

'Are we under arrest, then?' we shouted. The militia became flustered. 'Go indoors,' they ordered. The visitors looked on in perplexity. The militia escorted them out.

We went to the window to watch. The woman was protesting bitterly at the way they had been treated. When they saw us at the window they attempted to speak to us, but were dragged back. The little group gradually disappeared among muted angry protests from all sides.

Some officers attempted to move the church members away from the window, but they stood firm. The Securitate and militia made a half-hearted attempt to impose control again, but it was too late. As the anger of the crowd increased, its morale was growing visibly. A quarter of an hour later all the

Securitate got into their cars and left. It was eleven
o'clock.

For the first time in months, our front door was
unguarded. Almost immediately, people began
pushing into our apartment.

Lajos Varga: *At about half past ten I had returned to my
work place, intending to go back to the church later. But I
received a telephone call from the Securitate offices. 'Your
wife is here. You are to come immediately.' I was worried
that it might be because I was known to be a friend of Laszlo
Tokes. But it was a different matter; my wife had suffered a
miscarriage the previous week and the Securitate were
convinced that it had been a deliberate abortion, which
would have been a serious offence under Ceausescu's
regime. They did not believe my wife. I had been summoned for separate cross-examination. I provided a two-
page statement. Eventually they released me. But it was
half past one before I was back outside the church. I missed
seeing the Securitate leave.*

The church office is a long, narrow room with a table
running its full length. We received our visitors
there. There was a constant flow of people embrac-
ing us, congratulating us, and weeping with us. For
the first time we heard from some of our parishioners what their own experiences had been
while we had been confined to our home, and what
had been happening in the city during the past
weeks. They told us how they had prayed for us and
suffered with us in countless ways.

The steady trickle of food that had been arriving
all morning through the window became a flood.
All our visitors brought gifts. Within an hour we
had about fifteen kilos of meat, thirty litres of milk

and thirty loaves of bread. Some brought precious fresh fruit because Edit was pregnant and others brought bags of firewood.

In the middle of it all we managed to eat some lunch, the first time for weeks that we had been able to invite friends to eat with us in our home. Those who could not get into our apartment pressed closed to the wall beneath the study window.

Every half-hour or so I went to speak to them. 'Has anything happened yet?' they demanded. 'Are you safe? How is Edit?'

'She is fine,' I assured them. 'She is resting, because she is very tired.' But the crowd would not believe me and insisted that I brought her to the window so they could see for themselves.

So that heady, extraordinary morning came to an end. Edit and I were full of happiness, but there was a fear about which neither of us spoke. We were used to the way things happened in Romania. Always, after protests such as this, reprisals followed. It was inconceivable that the Securitate would give up, that they would not come back. Every minute that passed made the situation more serious.

Yet at the same time I felt a reckless optimism, a crazy hope that bloodshed might yet be avoided. *They can't possibly evict us now*, I thought. *There are too many people. Something will have to be sorted out. These people are prepared to stay all night if necessary*.

Inside, the celebrations continued in the tiny office. Outside, the crowd was growing.

Lajos Varga: *I returned at half past one. The crowd had increased dramatically. Now there were hundreds instead of dozens.*

The crowd was so large that the Securitate came and drove away from the front of the building a car that had been used as a temporary shelter for guards to keep warm between shifts. There was a danger that the vehicle might be damaged by the people.

I was standing some way back from the church. After being detained at the Securitate once already, I had no wish to be arrested. I had a good view of the study window and saw Laszlo Tokes appear every half-hour or so throughout the afternoon.

By now what was happening was unthinkable; an open demonstration of public feeling in support of an individual against the State. And still the Securitate stayed away.

You can only appreciate the bizarre tenseness of the scene when you remember that at that time in Romania, if you wanted to have a birthday party with ten guests you had to ask permission from the Securitate in advance. Somehow or other, the people had summoned the courage to gather in an illegal assembly. I consider that was the first step in the Revolution.

The second was the realisation that we had power. We were able to control what was happening. We had driven the Securitate away. It was like living a wild dream, a forbidden fantasy.

In the afternoon, the nature of the crowd changed. Now there were two distinct elements.

The first was our church members who had been with us from early morning, committed to support us and resist the eviction. The others were new-comers, drawn by the sight of a large crowd, and curious to know what was going on. News had spread all over the city. 'The pastor at the Reformed Church was going to be evicted – there's been a big demonstration – the Securitate tried to disperse the people but it was they who ran away . . .' And (I was told much later) as the afternoon wore on, people began to think things they had not allowed themselves to think for years: *This is the time. This is what we have been waiting for. We have to take the opportunity while it is still available.*

It had begun as an ethnic Hungarian demonstration, but by the afternoon many ethnic Romanians had joined us and soon outnumbered our small congregation. In the minds of many ethnic Hungarians, Romanians were synonymous with Ceausescu; his oppression was a Romanian nationalism and the Romanian state he was creating was the enemy of Hungarian cultural identity. So it was profoundly moving to see that by dusk most of the people outside were Romanians.

And during the afternoon students began to arrive, both Hungarian and Romanian. They were full of enthusiasm and determination and seemed to be quite organised.

Every half-hour I was called to the window. Edit remained in the office, welcoming visitors. The crowd demanded that I lead a service and preach to them. So I spoke briefly several times, in Hungarian and then in Romanian. 'We are one in Christ,' I said. 'We speak different languages, but we have the same Bible and the same God. These are unique times . . .'

Lajos Varga: *By now a large part of the crowd was there to protest against the government. It was no longer a silent protest by the Hungarian Reformed Church. Word had spread through the town that Laszlo Tokes was refusing to be evicted by the Securitate, and many had*

*come who had nothing to do with our church but wanted to
support Laszlo's stand against the regime.*

*Rumours were circulating in the crowd. For example,
some were saying that the Securitate car had been moved
earlier in order to encourage the people – to help the
demonstration gather force; that some of the Securitate
were secretly supporting the demonstration.*

*Fragments of information passed from person to person.
It was said that the secretary had returned to his office and
summoned all the members of the Nomenklatura – the
heads of all the State and local institutions, the inner circle
of the Party – and instructed them to wear the uniform of
the National Guard and launch a counterdemonstration
the next day if necessary.*

Through the afternoon I studied the crowd. From
the windows we could see individuals who were
acting as information points telling newcomers
what was happening and adding their own interpretations. A kind of folklore was already developing about the day's events; those who knew our
church supplied background information to those
who did not and already rumours and opinions
were rife.

And there were other individuals in the crowd too
– shadowy people who stood watching carefully.
Our visitors pointed some of them out to us. 'That
one, over there, by the tree . . . he's a plain-clothes
Securitate man; he came and questioned us a month
ago . . . and that woman near the corner, she's an
informer; we all know about her.'

It seemed that in the street you could see every
kind of person: the silent ones, those who stood
motionless staring at the window, those whose
faces bore an almost trance-like quality; and the

activists, the Securitate spies, and some we identified as provocateurs urging the crowd to violence.

For most of the day, people had been praying
openly in the street. Towards evening, they began
to sing hymns.

Lajos Varga: *There was tension, but still no violence. As
dusk fell in the late afternoon, people lit candles and placed
them on the wall, on the pavement, in the basement
windows. And waited.*

We had to do something to control the flow of
visitors. Edit had not slept for six nights, thanks to
exhaustion and worry. Now the excitement and
emotion of seeing so many friends had drained her
physically and emotionally and she was distraught.
Visitors thronged the office, a large part of the
crowd was standing in the main entrance hall and
on the steps outside our apartment, and we were
besieged by requests to allow people to spend the
night in our apartment. Many were strangers we
had never met.

The members of our presbytery and other friends
arranged a rota of people to man the entrance,
deciding who should be allowed in to see us and
also calming the crowd: 'There's nothing to see
inside . . . the Tokeses are tired, we should let them
rest a little now . . . Let's keep as quiet as possible so
we don't disturb them too much.'

But by nine o'clock the crowd was gripped by
excitement and was beyond my power to direct. I
was still the focus. If friends needed to leave, the
only way to clear a space at our front door was for
me to appear at one of the windows; whereupon the

crowd moved to see me and our visitors could slip away.

By now my appearances at the windows were appeals for calm. We had survived the day; the Securitate had not come back; now we just wanted to be quiet and take stock. 'Please,' I urged, 'we have finished for today. I won't be coming out again. Good night, and thank you! We will see what happens tomorrow.'

But as soon as I turned away from the window the chanting began again. 'Tokes! Laszlo Tokes! We want Laszlo Tokes! Come to the window, come to the window!' Suddenly I was afraid of the crowd; I wondered whether I could control them for much longer. Then the chanting became menacing as they demanded that I turn the study lights full on to give them illumination in the street. Also, there were some drunks in the crowd and some who were beginning to behave like hooligans.

Our visitors reported that the crowd intended to stay on the street all night. They planned to wait in shifts. We were moved by the massive show of support we had received but were full of foreboding about what the results would be. I went to the window for the last time.

'Please forgive me. We are grateful that you are here. Thank you from the bottom of my heart. But you must understand we are under terrible pressure. We must sleep. My wife is pregnant. She needs to be quiet. I am going to shut up the house now.'

It was ten o'clock. We closed the main gates of the church building, said good night to the friends who were guarding our front door, and had supper in the kitchen with a few close friends whom we had asked to stay the night with us. We hoped that the crowd would disperse, but there was no sign of that happening. Then we knew that we were in a potentially revolutionary situation. Where it might lead was anybody's guess.

Lajos Varga: *By now the crowd numbered over a thousand; more Romanians than Hungarians and many more than our own congregation. There were many Baptists from the church of Pastor Petru Dugulescu with whom our church had close ties. I recognised a number from the Pentecostal Church; earlier in the week I'd mentioned to their leader, a colleague of mine at work, what was going to happen on Friday, and had asked him to urge his congregation to come and support us. And they had come. And many more besides.*

'Look out of the window! There's a delegation!'

The message was shouted through from the front door. We were still in the kitchen, half an hour after locking the gates. Though the kitchen was normally too far away from the windows for street noise to be heard, we could hear loud shouting. We rushed to the window.

The delegation was composed of the town mayor and several colleagues. We watched as he unsuccessfully tried to disperse the crowd. Then he demanded to see us. The crowd responded angrily. 'You're going to evict them secretly; you've got soldiers in the basement; you're going to smuggle the pastor out. But we won't let you in!'

There was a real danger that the mayor might be lynched, so great was the anger of the crowd. I began to try to reason with the crowd from the window.

'I want to speak to these men and find out what they want.'

'No! Don't you see? They want to kidnap you. Don't let them in.'

'Dear brothers and sisters,' I said, 'we have to talk to them. We cannot solve anything without dialogue. Let's see what they want.'

After considerable discussion we came to an agreement. I promised not to allow myself to be abducted and to report the results of my conversation with the mayor to the crowd. They agreed to let him enter the building on condition that a delegation from the crowd came too as witnesses.

It was not the first meeting I had had with the local authorities that week. Two days earlier, the Inspector of Cults had come to see me. He was very amiable and courteous. Would I go to the town hall where the Party secretary, Mr Robu, wanted to meet me?

I said that if he was prepared to guarantee my safety I would go. I knew there could be no genuine guarantee, but also I had a feeling that there was no real danger, that this was not the time the Securitate had chosen to strike. And I was convinced that dialogue must be continued as long as possible.

Robu was a genial, bluff man. Coffee was brought in. The atmosphere was carefully polite.

'I'm concerned about the announcement you made from your pulpit on Sunday,' he said. 'You have asked your congregation to come to the church on Friday.' Neither of us bothered to explain how he had heard about it. The Securitate spies had done their job. 'Do you not think that there will be trouble? Why have you decided not to obey the decision of Bishop Papp? It is your duty to do so.'

'Because it is an illegal demand,' I said. 'I have no intention of obeying and have explained my reasons to the bishop many times.' *They can smell danger*, I realised. *They are afraid of a demonstration. They are afraid of the people*. 'This is the only way I can stand against it.'

The secretary beamed comfortably. 'You know, you can tell your congregation not to come. They really don't need to bother. Nothing is going to happen until Monday anyway.'

I raised my eyebrows. 'Indeed.'

'Well, the eviction order expires on Friday. So even if you do not leave, they will wait until the next day to come for you.' I must have looked sceptical. 'Yes, it is so. But the next day is a Saturday and nobody wants to work on a Saturday!' He grinned at his own joke. 'Then the next day – Sunday – and obviously they will not choose to interrupt divine service. So you see, it will be Monday before anything happens. You can tell your people to wait until then.'

It was an obvious trick. But even if I had wanted to do what he asked, it was impossible. 'There are no services in the church before Friday,' I pointed out. 'There is no way I could tell them.'

He rose, indicating that the meeting was at an end. He tried to summon up a look of regret. 'We are really very sorry that all this has happened, Pastor Tokes,' he said. 'Our hands are tied in the matter, of course. We have no links with the Securitate and we do not know why the bishop has taken the course he has chosen. We know you are a good man. But we cannot intervene.' He accompanied me to the door. 'We honour you for your work, you know.'

The smooth lies made no difference to me; I had
expected nothing else. It was not the first time the
town authorities had pretended to me that they had
nothing to do with the Securitate or denied that the
attacks on me and my family were anything at all to
do with them.

That had been Wednesday. Now it was Friday.
He had been proved wrong, I reflected, as I looked
out of the window at the vast murmuring congregation and the sea of flickering flames.

The mayor would not come into the apartment. His
party and the six people from the crowd came to the
half-landing outside my door. We stood in a circle.

He was a small, fat man in his sixties, swarthy-
skinned and very arrogant. 'What's happening
here? What is going on?' But he was already defeated. It was a victory for the crowd that the mayor
had been forced to come to the church; he was more
used to summoning people to his office and would
never have stirred himself to investigate grievances
of the Hungarian minority.

'The protest is over the illegal eviction of Pastor
Tokes.'

The mayor pretended to be astonished. 'But that
is not so. I know nothing of an eviction.' He spread
his hands helplessly. 'It is a rumour. It's quite
incorrect. There are no legal grounds for eviction.'
His manner became brisk and efficient. 'We will
issue you with a temporary permit to remain here.
You will need to renew it at the appropriate time. It
is a purely civil matter. It has nothing to do with the
bishop. Now, what other problems do you have?'

'We have no access to shops. We are forbidden
fuel. The authorities have broken all our windows.

Our door was broken when we were attacked by the Securitate.'

He promised everything. The windows would be replaced, the door would be repaired. All our grievances would be sorted out.

'And my wife's doctor has not been permitted to see her, despite the fact that she is pregnant and has not been in good health.'

The mayor feigned surprise. 'You shall have a doctor tomorrow,' he promised. 'And tomorrow all the other problems will be sorted out. So you see, you may now disperse the crowd that has gathered.' There was a veiled threat in his words, but we were helpless. 'I do not want a scandal,' I agreed.

The mayor turned to go. 'Fine,' he said. 'Tomorrow everything will be done.' He signed to an assistant. 'Now I must take the names of this delegation from the people.'

He brushed aside the protests. 'I am the mayor and these are my colleagues.' He introduced them each by name. 'Now I must have *your* names, so that we know who is party to our agreement.' His small rat-like face watched with pleasure as the names were taken. His jowls trembled with satisfaction. Later we discovered that each of the people whose names had been taken were arrested.

Lajos Varga: *Inside the house, the mayor and the small group who had gone in with him were deep in discussion with Laszlo Tokes.*

Eventually the mayor and his party emerged and went away. Laszlo appeared at the window and told us the promises that the mayor had made. The crowd were furious. 'Don't believe him! He's a liar! Don't trust a Communist!'

After the mayor left, the crowd quietened down a little. The house was shut up. People stamped their feet to warm them, and the numerous candles cast a watery yellow light over faces that were anxious and uncertain.

I closed the shutters. It seemed that the Securitate had decided to do nothing that day. Outside, a few people were singing hymns. Others began to chant quietly: 'Liberty! Liberty!'

We resolved to leave the windows closed until morning. We did not know that after the mayor left, plain-clothes Securitate men appeared from each end of the street and attacked the crowd with clubs. Soon there was only a core of about 150 people determined to stay all night. It was a simple matter for the Securitate to disperse them.

Inside the house we were finding it difficult to sleep. At one o'clock I went to the window again and looked out. In the deserted side street only the candle stumps remained from the mighty demonstration.

I leaned further out. In the main road, on the far side, fifteen or twenty people were keeping vigil, the candles in their hands glimmering like fireflies in the city gloom.

2

EARLY YEARS

Mention Transylvania to people in the West and most will think immediately of the dark forests, remote castles and restless undead of the Hollywood vampire films. But in reality, there are few castles in Transylvania. It is a region of rich fields and strikingly beautiful mountains, with innumerable villages and several historic cities. The roads even today carry little traffic, and drivers of fast cars are often forced to wait while a flock of sheep or cows move philosophically out of the way. Oxcarts and horse-drawn wagons reflect a more leisurely age, and the faces of the peasants who have grown old in the Transylvanian countryside are lined and worn with years of toil.

Transylvania is intimately involved in the history of Hungary of which it was part for 1,000 years. The Hungary-Romania border, once dramatically marked by the Transylvanian Alps and the Carpathians, now runs across the flat expanse of the Great Hungarian Plain. The region was occupied by the Romanian army in 1916, seceded from the Austro-Hungarian empire at the end of the war and was then annexed by the kingdom of Romania.

In the interwar period a Fascist terrorist organisation called the Iron Guard (an organisation similar in many ways to the modern Securitate) gained considerable power. In 1939 Romania remained neutral, but in 1940 entered the war on Germany's side. In 1944 the Iron Guard leadership was overthrown and Romania joined the Allies. Part of the negotiations included the recognition, after an Allied victory, of Romania's claim to Transylvania.

When I was born in Kolozsvar in northern Transylvania, on April 1st, 1952, the population of Transylvania was still largely Hungarian and memories of the postwar settlement still rankled. In a larger sense, Transylvania was only one of many regions that were casualties of the treaties that followed World War I: the Great Powers had attempted to break up the Austro-Hungarian empire, separate Germany and Austria and give sovereign statehood to each nationality. Thus the old empire was divided between seven states.

The results were tragic, and some of the legacy of the treaties made then is only becoming apparent today, as nationalist fervour and ethnic tension cause bitterness and bloodshed across Eastern Europe even in the wake of the momentous events of the winter of 1989–90.

Thousands of miles of new frontiers were created in Europe; barriers that cut across long-established human relationships, severed rail and road systems and took no account of the numerous minority populations within the new states. In Kolozsvar there was a large Hungarian population. My parents mother tongue was Hungarian, and they loved Hungarian culture, referred to their home city by its Hungarian name and preserved and continued the Hungarian Protestant traditions that had been bequeathed to the region by its generations of Hungarian inhabitants.

My father was a pastor in the Hungarian Reformed Church and was very poor. He had graduated from the Theological Institute at Kolozsvar in 1938, and in that year left Romania to study theology in Germany. Upon the outbreak of war he moved to Switzerland to continue his theological studies, returning in 1940 to Kolozsvar where he became the bishop's secretary. He was also appointed as a chaplain at the Theological Institute. In 1946, after the war, he was promoted within the department, but as the Communists were now in power and clergymen were despised, there was no great increase in income.

My parents lived with their six children in church accommodation in Kolozsvar, in one of a number of apartments that surrounded a quiet courtyard. When my father arrived at the maternity hospital to inspect his new son for the first time, he apologised to my mother because he had no money to buy flowers.

It had been a difficult and exhausting birth. My mother had a history of heart troubles made worse by the family's poverty. As a young boy I remember her regularly washing for her family of ten, pummelling wet clothes in the tub until two or three in the morning. Her health was so frail that when it was found that she was carrying an unusually large baby, doctors urged her to have an abortion for her own safety. She and my father talked and prayed about the matter, but it was never an option for them. 'This life in the womb has been given by

God,' explained my father, 'and therefore the child must be born.'

I emerged into the world weighing ten pounds. My mother's poor health during the pregnancy and the long and traumatic labour had taken their toll of me, and for several frantic minutes the nurses tried to start my heart beating. As was the custom, I was dipped alternately into basins of hot and cold water while my mother pleaded: 'Save my baby! I've worked so hard for him!'

And soon my mother was able to hold me in her arms – a large baby with an even larger head, staring at her with the enormous liquid brown eyes that our family is born with. When the time came to take me home to the apartment in the church compound, she and my father carried me in their arms. There was no money available for a taxi.

My childhood was a happy one, despite the initial welcome I received from my brothers and sisters, who pronounced me the ugliest child they had ever seen. They had some excuse; my large head tended to flatten on whatever side I slept, and I soon acquired the nickname 'Square-head'. Nor was the date of my birth overlooked; it was thought very amusing that I should be born on April Fools' Day, and I was often reminded of the fact. But we were a very close family, and the teasing was always good-natured. After a few years my odd looks became more normal, though in many family photographs of the period you can recognise me by my large head and larger eyes.

My mother remembers me as the most strong-willed of all her children, and recalls that my 'beautiful eyes' could gain me victory in any confrontation;

but I was brought up with a deep respect for the values of family life, and in that family life, Church and Christianity were interwoven so that it was impossible to tell where one ended and the other began. Indeed, one of the two major influences on my childhood was the sight of my father working at his desk, absorbed in his papers, surrounded by piles of books. The serenity on his face as he prepared his sermons and studied the Bible had a profound effect upon me, and at an early age I announced to anybody who listened that I was going to be a bishop when I grew up. The announcement was greeted, predictably, with good-humoured hilarity by my brothers and sisters: 'Bishops aren't born on All Fools' Day, Squarehead!'

Neither in my family nor in the circles in which we moved was there any exaggerated piety, a concentration on appointed times and duties. The Christianity in which I grew up was a very natural human environment. It was not considered important that there should be a particular time of day at which you opened your Bible, and that after reading for a certain period of time you then shut it, and the same for praying. For many people that is helpful, and I would not want to suggest that they should not do it. But for us, the Christian faith was similar to a folk custom – by which I mean that it was an integral part of our lives. We were taught to read and know the Bible, and our parents taught us to apply it; a family crisis, a decision that needed to be made, a moment of perplexity might all prompt my parents to quote a sentence from the Bible or one of the teachings of Jesus. Nor were such quotations merely automatic; they were thoughtfully chosen, a deliberate application of the biblical truths to the situation in hand.

Even our own history was viewed in biblical terms. For example, when we read of the fall of Babylon in the Bible, we remembered our great national tragedies, such as the fall of the Hungarian kingdom in 1526 at the Battle of Mohacs, the decisive great confrontation between the Hungarians and the Turks; the Massacre of Made (1754), a small village in Transylvania; and the suffering caused in Transylvania during the reign of the Rakoczis, by the Austrians in 1644 and 1705 and the Turks in 1660. When, years later, the full horror of Ceausescu's regime became clear, we recognised him as an Antichrist, an example of the destroyers of the people of God foretold in the prophecies of the Bible.

The Reformed faith was an important strand in our Hungarian heritage. Though the Reformation flourished in Hungary under the threat of the Turkish invaders – to the extent that at the end of the sixteenth century a Hungarian Catholic bishop bewailed the fact that for every Catholic in the country there were a thousand Protestants – the Protestant communities of Hungary suffered during the Counter-Reformation under the Habsburgs. Western Hungary was forcibly converted to Catholicism, the number of Protestants was reduced to one-third of the population and Transylvania in the east became a heartland of the Reformation faith.

The tragedies of the Hungarian people were part of the fabric of my earliest childhood. We had no radio in my home when I was born; we were too poor for such luxuries. But in 1956 when the Soviets invaded Hungary, my father borrowed money to buy a radio to listen to the news. It is one of my first childhood memories – sitting with my family, listening to the hourly reports on what was happening, imagining the tanks rolling into the great city and the bullets and shells. For the first time I understood the reality of a great power oppressing a small community. I was four years old.

My mother taught us Bible stories. Prayer was something that was a response to everyday experience. There was not a day in our home when the worlds of faith and the everyday did not touch each other. In later life my fellow ministers sometimes criticised me for my lack of apparent piety. But for my family and my people, religion was never something separate from life. Christianity is to be practised as well as meditated upon. I prefer the pragmatism of Anglo-Saxon Christianity, for example, to the high principles of German theology.

For the same reason, I cannot look back on my Christian life and isolate distinct stages and levels of maturity. It was an organic process. I was taught the truths of the Christian faith from my birth, was given the priceless privilege of being raised in a Christian home, was nurtured by a loving Christian family and our Christian friends and relatives in the villages and had several examples of godly men and women in my family. In truth, I cannot look back to a time when I was not a Christian.

The second influence was the Transylvanian village of Szepkenyeruszentmarton, near Dej, where members of my mother's family had lived for generations. The name means 'St Marton of the good bread': we usually shortened it to 'Szentmarton'.

It was in that village that my grandfather came to work as pastor. By the time he went there, long

before Ceausescu had begun his plans to 'assimi-
late' forcibly the Hungarian community, the entire
village, historically Hungarian, had virtually forgotten the old language and customs.

He distributed Hungarian books and set up a
village library, and by these and other methods did
much to raise the cultural level of the village. And at
the same time, he raised the spiritual level. Protestant Christianity and Hungarian culture were one
and the same in that village, and my mother, who
was born there, grew up with a religious understanding of the wholeness of life that she in turn
passed on to me and to the rest of her children.
'Your grandfather did many good things in Szentmarton,' she told us. 'He helped many people with
their problems, and when the people had almost
lost their Hungarian identity and become Romanians, he showed them how to be Hungarians
again.'

In 1940, when northern Transylvania briefly returned to Hungary, there was starvation in Szentmarton. In those days the village pastors were also
leaders of the village. My grandfather went to Hungary and brought back grain in large quantities by
train and gave it to the people. He was recognised as
a public figure involved with the economics of village life but also respected as a pastor and counsel-
lor. He gave advice on many subjects to all who
asked. Like many of his clerical contemporaries, he
was a patriarchal figure in his community.

He was not the only example of godly pastoring in
my family. Another grandfather was a dean in
Malnas, who rose high in the Church hierarchy but
never lost his commitment to the people to whom
he had been called to minister.

When I became a teenager I decided to visit Szent-marton for myself. Perhaps the stories my mother had told, the wonderful anecdotes of my grand-father's kindness and the preservation of the Hungarian way of life in a small Romanian village, were just wishful thinking, half-remembered fanta-sies coloured by sentiment and affection. I needed to see the village with my own eyes.

So I made the trip with a group of friends, and I discovered as I met various members of my family living in the village, that what my mother had told me was true. I never met my grandfather, for he died in 1952, the year I was born. But the Tokeses had made an impact on Szentmarton. And I observed there something that is common to many aspects of Transylvanian Protestant history – the similarity to the history of Israel. In that village there was no artificial distinction between religion and secular. The two were intertwined, just as they were in Israel, and in calling the people to be conscious of their national identity and customs, my grandfather was urging them to take heed for their souls.

I began to spend my summer holidays in the village, living with my relatives. Each day I went into the fields with the peasants, imitating every-thing they did and tackling all the jobs I was asked to do. Of course I was not paid for this work; I did it for my own enjoyment. But at the age of fourteen I was presented with a certificate by the mayor of the village. It stated that I had shown myself capable of doing the work of middle-aged peasants.

In a very real sense, it was an education. The experiences and impressions I gained for myself, and the knowledge I had of the struggles of my

grandfathers on behalf of the people, prepared me
for what I was going to be as an adult.

The twin images which influenced my childhood
were to become the guiding principles of my life.
The image of my father studying, praying and preparing to preach to his congregation represented
the centrality of the Bible – the importance of being
close to God, the truth that however impressive you
might be in the eyes of the world and however high
you might rise in the hierarchy of the Church, if
your heart was not right and your knowledge of
God was imperfect, it all added up to nothing.

But side by side with that image, balancing it and
completing the whole, was the image of the trim
fields and gentle slopes of Szentmarton, the Hungarian people and their way of life. For I realised at a
very young age that religion was not something that
could be kept inside books. If Christianity was not
part of everyday life – if it did not, indeed, provide
the meaning, values and centre of everyday life – it
was sterile and useless.

The people of the village demonstrated that well.
For them, church was at the centre and the Bible was
the prevailing force in their hard and laborious lives.

And they did work very hard. I rose at dawn to go
with them to the fields, and we worked all day. I
was given no privilege as a member of the pastor's
family; if privilege there was, it was the privilege of
being beloved by the whole village, of being treated
as one of their own sons.

In the evenings and on Sundays, I joined in the
life of the village. I attended services in the church
and read extensively. The results of my grandfather's efforts were clear to see in the village; there

was a much higher level of literacy and interest in books than in any other village I knew. The villagers read widely and knowledgeably. And they read the Bible, not out of duty, but out of a desire to understand better the book that was at the centre of their lives.

Though we were Hungarians living in territory which had been taken from Hungary, we were not revolutionaries. I did not as a child dream about taking up arms and restoring Transylvanian to Hungary. But Magyar culture was under threat in our villages and towns and Hungarian history was not taught in the Romanian schools.

In one sense I was fortunate in my schooling. In the 1950s and 1960s Hungarians or in some cases Germans were still in the majority in the chief cities of Transylvania; the forced migration that Ceausescu was to introduce later was still in the future. So there were still a few schools in Kolozsvar that originated in Hungarian Protestantism, though the policy of the government was to make the language and culture of Romania compulsory for the whole country.

I attended a primary school that had once been a Hungarian Reformed school. When I reached secondary school age, there were still three Hungarian-speaking 'gymnasiums' or secondary schools in Kolozsvar. My parents chose a secondary school that had been founded by Hungarian Catholics, so I was able at least to speak the language with young people of my own age. In both schools there were some teachers who remembered the past, who treasured the spirit of Transylvania, and they sometimes took the opportunity to talk to us in

secret, instructing us in religion and giving us tanta-
lising glimpses of the time when Transylvania had
been within the Hungarian borders. But such moments were rare and were not approved at all by the
authorities.

So each day my mother taught stories about the
great kings and heroes of the past. Men such as
Dugonics Titus who sacrificed himself defending a
Hungarian castle against the Turkish invaders. He
embraced the leading soldier who was about to
plant the Turkish flag on the battlements and
jumped to his death with him into the moat far
below. As my mother told us this story she waved
her arms and jumped up and down in her excitement. All her stories lived vividly in our minds, and
I grew up with a fierce pride in my Hungarian
nationality. When I was fourteen I wrote a poem
that was so full of nationalist fervour that my
mother was afraid it would cause problems for me
when I was known to be the author. 'You ought to
burn this poem,' she advised. I shook my head. 'I
didn't write it so that I could burn it,' I retorted, with
a characteristic gesture of my head. (My mother tells
the story, on the other hand, of my coming to her
one day with a poem that had moved me deeply.
'Look at this poem, read it – isn't it beautiful?' I
asked. Then, half-teasing – 'It is written by an ethnic
Romanian, you know.' She says it proves I was a
lover of justice even in my childhood.)

But as I grew older, I had many opportunities to
learn that loving a nation meant much more than
simply glorying in its past or defending its rights.
For a Christian, to love a nation meant to care for its
people. A strong influence on me was a Hungarian
pastor, Janos Herman, who ministered to people

living in remote villages. He was an elderly man, suffering from a goitre condition and in frail health. Yet he worked as hard as everybody else in the fields in all weathers and tending the animals. I have never forgotten seeing Janos Herman, often far from well, walking across mountains to visit five or six of his countrymen to preach the Gospel to them.

Such generosity, and the attention that Janos and my grandparents paid to people's material as well as spiritual needs, was not mere philanthropy. In the West, there is often a charity that extends to giving food and water to starving people but takes no account of the spiritual life or the life of the community in which the individual lives. The concept of 'the rights of the individual' has always sounded somewhat strange to me. Individualism is a kind of alienation; and in many parts of the world, community has been lost as individuality has thrived. Nor do I find in the Bible much emphasis on the solitary Christian, the lone hero of the faith separate from the community of the people of God.

In Szentmarton and in my own home, I learned the meaning of the image of the pastor as shepherd of the flock. As I grew older, it was the concept of the flock – the village, the city, the people of Zion, Transylvania, Romania – that formed the core of my ministry.

One of our Hungarian poets has written, 'Though he be a thief, he is still Hungarian, he is still one of your own.' And how can a pastor make distinctions and say, 'This one is worthy of love, but that one is not'? I feel deeply for individuals and much of the work of any pastor involves ministering to people on their own. But each person is part of his or her community and must be ministered to as such. As an English poet has said, 'No man is an island.'

We were a family of strong willpower and strong characters. I and my brothers and sisters were not reluctant to tell other people about our faith, and as we grew up we looked for jobs that would bring us into contact with people. My sister, for example, became a dentist, and often talked to her patients about the gospel. 'You need to find out about God,' she advised them. 'Go to church; that is where you will discover the truth about him.' One of my brothers became a physicist, regarded his field of study as a mission field and took every opportunity to talk to colleagues. Another sister, Erzsebet, is a teacher who distributes food and medicine to the needy.

My parents, who believed profoundly in the power of Christianity to change people and through them the society in which they lived, were delighted to see their children taking their stand for the gospel in the secular world. But my mother secretly longed that one at least of her sons would become a pastor. She never put pressure upon us and showed no disappointment at all as one by one her sons chose vocations in other fields. But it was a very special moment for her when, in my mid-teens, after one of the holidays I had spent with a pastor and his family, I came to her and announced: 'I am going to be a pastor.'

The main factors in my decision were the example of my family, particularly my father, and the experience of working with people, particularly in Szentmarton. From my own experiences and from watching pastors at work, I gained the image of the shepherd watching over his flock. That has always been for me the central image of pastoral work and it is one that is drawn from the Bible and from life itself.

That model has always been important to me, and it was a concrete one; in my village holidays, for example, I actually worked as a shepherd. When I returned to Szentmarton for the first time after I had become a minister, and preached in the village church, I began: 'You see, my brethren and sisters; in my childhood I was a shepherd in your village, but now I have returned as a shepherd of souls!'

It was not simply a choice of career. For me, becoming a pastor was something that God called me to. As I grew older, I saw that not all pastors were like those in my family. I saw pastors, for example, who were often drunk; they were not living for God, but off him.

Some were worldly, some were lazy, some had long since chosen to serve the Communist regime instead of the kingdom of God. I became very dissatisfied with the condition of the Church. I listened carefully to sermons and ecclesiastical pronouncements and gradually developed a conviction that I wanted to spend my life serving God in the Church and try to fight against some of the abuses and wrongs that I saw.

In a sense to become a pastor was an uncharacteristic decision for me. I hated the 'pastor dynasties' where children of pastors had entered the priesthood themselves because their parents had put pressure on them. That was one reason why we had so many bad pastors.

During my last years at school, I held fast to my call

to be a pastor against other possibilities, each of which exerted its own pull. There was open opposition to the idea; the official atheistic education policy did not recognise the Christian ministry as a useful career, and the director of my school laughed in my face when he heard of my ambition. Many pupils in Romanian schools who hoped to enter the Church kept their plans a secret.

In my final year, at the age of seventeen, I was torn between becoming a teacher and becoming a pastor. I had an excellent English teacher, a Jewish woman who brought love and sensitivity to her work. She made no distinction between Christians and Jews and in a way she identified with the sufferings of the Hungarian minority. I had a great love for literature and the attractions of teaching were strong. As a pastor in a marginalised community working with small and often demoralised congregations, what could I do? On the other hand, as a Christian teacher I would be ideally placed to guide and influence young people.

In that year, too, I had a rare confrontation with my father. I had become very diligent in bringing my friends to church, and a small group of friends joined my family each Sunday. At that time, my father was an assistant minister. When he was deputy bishop of Kolozsvar, he did not preach Sunday sermons because he was not a parish minister. But now he preached every Sunday and he expected all his children to attend. The call to the ministry had not turned me into a saint; I was a teenager, liable to the phases of rebellion and independence that all teenagers go through.

The confrontation erupted one beautiful sunny Sunday morning. We were preparing to go to church as usual when my friends turned up dressed in casual clothes.

'Hey, Laszlo! It's too hot to go to church today. We're going swimming. Why don't you come with us? Change into something more comfortable – hurry!'

I wriggled in my Sunday clothes, and hesitated. We had all gone to church together for several weeks now, but this was the first really hot Sunday we'd had.

'Come on, Laszlo – you can go to church any Sunday.'

I made a decision. 'Wait,' I said. 'I'll change.'

When I came out of my room dressed in my casual clothes and carrying my swimming things rolled up in a towel under my arm, my mother was scandalised and my brothers and sisters gasped in horrified amusement. My father had already gone on ahead to the church.

I adopted a relaxed air. 'You go on,' I said to my mother. 'I'm not going to church this Sunday. I want to go swimming with my friends today.'

She shook her head vigorously. 'Go and change your clothes,' she retorted. 'We are going to church – as we do every Sunday.'

Our eyes locked. For a moment I stared at her in mutinous anger. She held my gaze steadily. I looked away.

I went and changed back to my church clothes and went with my family to the service. I sang the hymns mechanically and heard nothing of the sermon. When we returned home, my father told me what he thought of my behaviour.

Afterwards my mother tried to heal the breach, but I remained cold and formal. After a few days matters improved, but I was unable to make the first move to repair the hostility between us. A few weeks later, I said to her, 'I've changed my mind. I don't want to be a pastor any more.'

A look of great sorrow passed over her face. I knew I had hurt her and was desperately sorry; but I didn't know how to put matters right.

For the next few weeks I went to church as usual, and for most of the time family relationships went back to normal. But inside, I was deeply unhappy. I was not at all sure that I had abandoned my desire to be a pastor. But I felt inadequate to be one; how could I teach and counsel other people when I had problems in my own life?

Eventually the crisis resolved itself. My mother, I knew, was praying fervently for me, and I myself was spending many hours thinking and praying about my situation. I was with my mother in the kitchen when one of my friends called to see me. We chatted together while my mother prepared the evening meal, standing at the stove with her back towards us.

After a few minutes of conversation, my friend asked me, half-teasing, 'Now, come on, Laszlo – what are you going to do with your life? What are your plans? What are you going to be?'

Later my mother told me that at that point she held her breath. What would her son answer? She didn't dare to move, but stood at the stove praying silently.

With some surprise I heard myself answer, 'I'm going to study at the Theological Institute here at Kolozsvar. I'm going to train to be a pastor.'

At the stove my mother began to weep, though she kept her back to us so we could not see, and silently gave thanks. 'Thank you, Lord. And I'm deeply, deeply grateful for this change of heart in my son.'

Such periods of rebellion against my parents' authority were brief. I place them in the category of those intergeneration conflicts that every family goes through. The fact that they were few and infrequent is an indication of the exceptionally happy family home in which I passed my childhood and teenage years.

Kolozsvar Theological Institute was the only Reformed theological college in Romania. Until the end of the nineteenth century there was a theological institution at Aiud, which was the capital of Transylvania in the days of the Hungarian reformed princes in the sixteenth and seventeenth centuries. At the end of the nineteenth century the theological department was moved to a new building in Kolozsvar, built in 1896 to mark the millennium of the Hungarian state. Only a secondary school remained at Aiud. So though the Theological Institute had been in Kolozsvar for a relatively short time, it was considered an ancient Reformed institution of Transylvania.

It was a famous institute with a great tradition. But in the 1950s it was destroyed. The building remained, but the Communist regime made wholesale changes to the staff. Godly theologians and scholars who had trained generations of students in the truths of the Reformed faith and the dynamics of the Christian life were thrown out of their posts. In their place the regime installed its own puppets, weak conformists who were appointed and paid by the State. They were compromised before they entered the classroom. They were teachers without moral or professional commitment.

These were the men who were in charge of the Theological Institute in 1971 when I walked through the entrance with its fine ornamental painted ceiling, showing sadly the results of years of neglect.

I enjoyed student life, but the quality of the teaching was appalling. There was no time to study on one's own or to follow up theological interests that were not on the syllabus. In some months there were as many as twenty examinations, and the course covered so many disciplines that it was impossible to gain a footing in them all, let alone master them and deepen our knowledge.

The whole timetable was taught using outdated teaching methods and the reason was obvious. It was never intended that the students should leave the institute properly equipped to preach God's word and pastor God's people. The strenuous examination schedule was deliberately demoralising.

The teaching staff were simply inadequate. They were incapable of teaching Christianity as a faith that transformed lives and societies. They succeeded in presenting Jesus Christ as a mere theological topic because they had no personal knowledge of him. They analysed the Church as a cult because the doctrine of the Bride of Christ meant nothing to them.

Many anecdotes were told about them. One visiting professor was said to have obtained his post because on a visit to the institute one day he wandered into the pulpit by mistake. Another tried to teach New Testament Greek. What made his lectures become legends was the fact that he used an antiquated textbook in which each line of Greek was followed by its Hungarian equivalent. Writing Greek examples on the blackboard, he often missed a line and wrote the wrong Hungarian words beneath. It was quite apparent that his knowledge of Greek was minimal.

The staff were men who would have been rejected in the parishes. With only one or two exceptions, they were the worst pastors in the Hungarian Reformed Church. One had been an officer in the Department of Cults in Bucharest, two others had jobs in the Communist government when it first came to power. In the early days it was useful to the regime to have such men, and the only people who would take on the work of being officers of an atheistic regime were the weakest, most conformist pastors.

When Communism later entered a new phase, the old guard were thrown out. Their puppet priests were thrown out with them and given other jobs. Most ended up at the Theological Institute as professors. It was a corrupt administration. The sons of the professors were given transparently preferential treatment, and when members of the staff resigned, the sons of professors automatically took their place. To their other abuses of the Church, the Communists added nepotism.

When I came to the institute I realised that the same opportunities were open to me. As a pastor's son, my destiny was to have a comfortable existence as a clergyman. When, in 1973, my father was appointed a professor of the institute and also deputy bishop, my options increased accordingly. Now all the doors would be open to me and the regime would possess me.

But I was not prepared to accept the opportunity. I wanted nothing handed down from the officials. I wanted to be able to say that what I did with my life was my own choice, not the result of accepting help, especially from the regime. Also I was determined that I would never marry a pastor's daughter. Our home and way of life were very different to the life lived by many weak and compromised pastors whom I knew, and marrying a pastor's daughter would have gone a long way to creating the kind of pastoral dynasty I hated.

When I began my studies at the institute, I lived at home and made the short journey there each day on foot. But after a while I went to my parents and said, 'I'd like to move into a dormitory at the university.' Students at the institute usually referred to it as 'the university', because its degree-awarding status was under threat from the regime.

'Why?' asked my mother. 'It's so expensive – it costs 500 lei a month, and it would be very difficult for us to find that extra money.' She indicated the cheerful sitting room with the familiar paintings on the walls, piles of books and our well-worn and well-loved family possessions. 'It's hardly any distance, you have a good place to sleep here and you can eat here easily. Why go to all the extra expense?'

I answered confidently, 'I want to live with the other students. We need to be together to make a stand.'

My mother understood. She had lived through my father's sufferings at the hands of the regime and understood that a strong student body at the

Theological Institute would be a very positive development. She was prepared to make the sacrifice. She gave her consent.

The need for the student body to have an identity and a voice was becoming very clear. In the late 1960s and early 1970s the Romanian government's pressure against the Hungarian population was beginning to intensify. Its record of persecution against other churches was well known. The forced removal of the Eastern Rite Catholic Church a few years before I was born, the persecution of the Orthodox sect, the Lord's Army, and the troubles which almost all mainline Romanian churches were experiencing had been a regular topic in our family's conversation and prayers for as long as I could remember.

After a period of restraint in the mid-1960s during which many people in the country became Christians and there was a genuine revival of faith in many areas, the pressures on the churches began again. It was forbidden to preach in public; new church buildings could only be built with official permission which was hardly ever granted; and existing churches could only display small signs to indicate that they were churches.

Individual Christians suffered numerous harassments. All Romanians were closely monitored and details of their visitors were kept on file. The churches were not permitted to give overnight hospitality to foreign visitors. The vast resources of Christian books and magazines that believers in Western countries take for granted did not exist in Romania where Christian literature was tightly controlled. Opportunities for printing further supplies were very few. It was prohibited for churches

to use photocopiers, and nothing could be printed
for church use or distribution until both text and
illustrations had been approved by the State.

At the same time, there was a rapid deterioration in
the situation of the Hungarian community in
Transylvania. The 'assimilation' policy of Ceausescu's government meant a systematic attack upon
our culture and our language. The old Hungarian
names for the cities were removed from maps;
Kolozsvar, Nagyvarad and Temesvar were replaced
by Cluj, Oradea and Timisoara. These were names
we knew and often used ourselves, but now they
were compulsory and the Hungarian names
appeared on the maps on longer.

Our daily life was affected in many ways. Before,
my mother could go shopping knowing that she
would meet many Hungarians and have many
opportunities to speak her own language. Now
fewer and fewer such opportunities existed as the
government began to displace communities. It was
rumoured that a secret ministry had been established in Bucharest with the sole function of overseeing the mass dispersal of people; for example,
the resettling of three or four million ethnic
Romanians from the Old Kingdom into the main
centres of the Hungarian areas.

Nagyvarad, Kolozsvar, Tirgu-Mures, Satu-Mare,
Brasov, Sibiu, Temesvar – most of these had had an
eighty per cent Hungarian population, but now the
government began to settle Romanians there. It was
not just Hungarians whose communities were
being changed by force; the Romanians who were
wrenched out of their own homes and moved to
cities hundred of miles away also suffered. Nobody

knew the exact numbers of those being resettled; the statistics are secret even today.

But the results are all too clear to see. I began my childhood in a community with a seventy per cent Hungarian population. Today it is seventy per cent Romanian. The turn-around has happened, not by natural movement of people and communities, but by a cynical use of one long-established people against their will in order to destroy the culture and life of another.

By the time I began at the Theological Institute, the pattern was emerging. My father was already known as a courageous and outspoken critic of the regime. For years he campaigned against the State's ruling that only a handful of people be allowed to train for the ministry annually. He wrote carefully considered papers arguing that the yearly intake did not begin to compensate for the natural wastage, the pastors lost to the Church through death and retirement.

I admired my father for his fearless stand. When I entered the Theological Institute, I found myself engaged in the first of my own conflicts with the regime.

3

KOLOZSVAR, BRASOV, DEJ – THE EARLY STRUGGLES

The poison that was gnawing at the heart of the Hungarian Reformed Church was a kind of schizophrenia. The regime was manipulating the teaching staff of the only theological institute, but more than that – at every point of leadership in the Church there was a duplication. A hierarchy of atheistic Church leaders, Ministry officials both from Bucharest and local, and regional inspectors all shadowed the ordained leadership.

And so every decision about the governing of the Church had to be made on two levels – the Church level and that of the State. Church government only continued because the State chose to allow it to do so. The bishops compromised; they sought the wishes of the State and adjusted their own activities to comply. The double accountability ran all the way down the Church structures. In most churches, decisions were in effect made not by the pastor and presbytery but by the atheistic regime.

At the Theological Institute in Kolozsvar there were two students with whom I became friends: the son of Gyula Nagy, Bishop of Transylvania; and Janos

Molnar, who was driven by a passion for reform of the institute. Together, we three decided to do something about the desperate situation in the Church. We refused to follow the prescribed path of clergy sons.

To prepare ourselves we went into the mountains for a week's retreat. We stayed in a small cottage and discussed the problem from every viewpoint we could think of. Our prayers together were very specific. Some of our friends had urged us to pray for the institute, that God would persuade our leaders to be good leaders. And, of course, that was always our Christian hope, but when the three of us met together we wanted God to show us a specific plan of action.

It should be said that we had an advantage in that our fathers were in power in the Church. They did not give us special favours, but we had a natural safeguard which would enable us to be more radical than we could otherwise have been. We wanted to take advantage of our privileged position to achieve reform.

As the week progressed we began to shape our strategy.

First, we wanted a properly elected student body to be allowed in the institute. It should have some executive status in the spirit of Western democracy. The institute was ruled unilaterally. The professors wanted to keep us quiescent and submissive, so they put their favourites in positions of leadership. The student president and the cultural secretary were both appointed by the teaching staff.

One of the decisions that emerged from that week of prayer and discussion was that we should propose changes in the electoral system. The existing method was that representatives of the students were invited to the director's office where they were handed a list of candidates they were permitted to propose.

Our approach was pragmatic. We used the system to gain positions within the student body, and then we used those positions to bring about change. We were explicit in our criticism of the system. We wanted to know why there were inadequate stocks of study books, why we were not allowed to have unrestricted student meetings, and many other things.

The board of professors was so shocked by our initiative that they suspended Janos for a year. They told us we were disobedient and threatened disciplinary action. But despite the attitude of the authorities, gradually things did begin to change. In a few years, student life was dramatically different.

The changes attracted the interest of the Securitate. The regime noted that something different was happening and the professors, aided by the Securitate, began to put pressure on the students. There were plain-clothes men in our classrooms and numerous spies, some of them members of the student body. When the Securitate wanted to interview a student, the order came through the institute office. The rector would receive a telephone call demanding that the student be sent to Securitate headquarters.

They never called me for interview or interrogation, though several from my circle of friends were summoned. But I was certainly under observation, as I discovered when I took up my first post.

I completed my studies in 1975, and in my last year was elected Student President.

In the Hungarian Reformed Church, theological students are required to spend two years in a training post after completing their formal studies. When I and my friends discussed our strategy for changing the Church, we looked at the Church as a whole and tried to decide where change was most achievable. The smallest deanery in the diocese of Kolozsvar was Brasov, a city to the east of Kolozsvar in a predominantly German area of Romania.

We decided that we would apply to go to Brasov when we finished our studies. We could influence the deanery and use our position to start the renewal of the Church there. This we did, and I was appointed a chaplain as were several others of my circle of friends.

A month after I arrived, I was called to the Securitate headquarters.

'We wished to make your acquaintance, Mr Tokes. Welcome to Brasov.'

The civilities carried no conviction. The Securitate officer opened a large folder. 'It is only right to warn you, Mr Tokes, that your reputation has come to Brasov ahead of you.' He leafed through the documents. 'Apparently you are something of a nationalist. And a mystic, too. A man of faith.' He gave me an unpleasant look.

The implicit threat in his words did not escape me. At that time, any form of piety was regarded as the most dangerous form of religion by the State. Since the fifties, pious pastors had been persecuted and Church authorities collaborated in the persecution. Pastor Richard Wurmbrand, the Romanian Baptist pastor, was imprisoned for fourteen years

between 1948 and 1962, and there were many more.
The attacks on believers were still going on. Later,
pressure was brought to bear against nationalist
religions, so I was doubly suspect.

'There are reports here,' said the officer.

'What reports are they?'

He began telling me what was in the folder. It was
a complete dossier about me, covering the past four
years. The Securitate had been observing me ever
since I entered the Theological Institute.

'Let us consider this report,' he said. 'It says that
at the institute you preached sermons.'

'It was required,' I explained. 'It was part of the
examination. Everybody had to preach a sermon in
front of staff and fellow students.'

'Well, let's see what you chose to preach about,
Mr Tokes. Hebrews chapter 13, fourteenth verse:
"Here we do not have an enduring city, but we are
looking for the city that is to come."' He paused
significantly. 'Well?'

'I don't see what the difficulty is.'

'The difficulty, Mr Tokes, is that it's hardly the
choice of a loyal Romanian citizen. Why did you tell
the students that their country is not Romania?
Which country do you consider they *do* belong to,
Mr Tokes?'

'But that's ridiculous! The meaning of the text is
quite clear. The apostle is using it in a quite different
sense. Neither Hungary nor Romania is my country
in that sense, but heaven. He is speaking of a
spiritual realm, and that is how I expounded it.'

It was a common Securitate technique to seize on
any possible ambiguity and interpret it as detri-
mental to the regime. But the chief reason for the
summons was that they wished to intimidate me at

the outset of my ministry. They did this with every pastor when he first began his work. Often the pastors were beaten during the interview.

It was a profoundly disillusioning experience for me. I realised from the comments made to me at the headquarters that there must have been informers among my fellow students, and that my professor had handed a full transcript of the sermon to the authorities.

In Brasov there were two Reformed Churches and a chapel. My job was to be assistant to the two pastors. Most of my time was spent preaching in one or other of the churches or further afield. There were about thirty places in the region that had no church congregation, just fifty or so Christians without a church. I preached constantly in this mission field. This was a predominantly German community living in a historically German area, but many Hungarian Reformed people had settled there, and my job as a chaplain was to care for them and minister to them.

During those two years, I and my fellow chaplains preached in a bewildering variety of places; in people's homes, in the German evangelical churches, in the open air. The German evangelicals were very kind to us and gave us the use of their buildings. One activity which was a foretaste of my future interests was leading the young people's Bible hour.

They were two happy years, despite the attentions of the Securitate. I had a good relationship with the Brasov pastors and a job to do that was clearly necessary. There were many opportunities for enjoying poetry and music, and I made good friends there. But when the two years were up it was time to move on.

One of the places in which I often preached was the town of Dej, and I had enjoyed my contacts with the believers there. The presbytery knew me well. When in 1977 my two years at Brasov came to an end, there were no full-time posts available and the Dej presbytery invited me to become an assistant pastor there. There was a deacon who occupied the pastor's post but there was more than enough work for an assistant.

A large part of my time at Dej was spent working with the young people. I started a Bible group, mainly of students; it was intended as the next step after confirmation. We had about 120 members and met weekly. The response was extremely encouraging, because you could have counted the number of Bible study groups in the entire Church on the fingers of both hands. Of course, it provoked the authorities.

The aim of our Bible group was to study and discuss the Bible together. Young people's attitude to the Scriptures was influenced strongly by the double perspective of the Communist State; what they heard from the pulpit was compromised by what the government told them, for example in the comments of State-appointed teachers of religion in the schools. But I wanted to help the young people to begin to form a distinctively biblical world-view that would cut across the double-mindedness that was destroying our society and our Church. It was like a deep chasm that had to be crossed, created by years of strong State propaganda and a weak, conformist Church hierarchy.

We set out to bring the Bible to bear on every aspect of daily life. I was trying to rebuild among the young people of Dej that seamless integration between faith and life that I had seen in my childhood summer holidays at Szentmarton and in my own family. So we grappled with developing a biblical view on science, art, the natural world, sociology, and many more aspects of life.

The meetings were based on discussion. The young people themselves chose the topic for each week and one person would lead the discussion, which usually became animated and very free. That in itself struck a blow against the regime's indoctrination. Dialogue and discussion were virtually unknown in the activities sponsored by the regime; teaching was entirely one-way. The Party secretary, the professor, the pastor, the preacher, all provided their unilateral interpretations, and there was no opportunity for discussion. Consequently people never learned to test what was said, to analyse arguments, to discover the truth for themselves.

As the meetings developed, we expanded our activities. I started an English language Bible hour in which only conversation in English was permitted. I wanted to teach the gospel and the English language at the same time.

Another innovation was a series of sessions in which members volunteered to be the subject of an evening's intense scrutiny. First somebody in the group would construct a portrait of that person drawn from personal knowledge, school activities, mistakes the person had made and even sins committed. Then other members would construct a case for the defence and the person himself would contribute his own statements. The purpose of it all was to demonstrate how inadequately we know ourselves and the impact we make on other people, and how until we look into the mirror of the gospel, we never truly repent of anything and are unable to change our hearts.

This was again a denial of the humanism we were taught in Communist schools, and the popularity of such meetings was duly noted by those whose job it was to observe secretly the new assistant pastor.

In the Bible, there is one book, Esther, where the name of God is never mentioned. Various explanations are offered why this should be. For example, it was pointed out that it was considered a sin to pronounce the name of God in its entirety.

I interpret it differently. We should not strive to have the name of God on our lips every moment. We do not need to talk about God constantly so much as to live in him, so that his name lives in every part of our life. Even though we may not be talking about God, or consciously acting as his spokesman at a particular time, we must act on every occasion as if God is actually using us as his mouthpiece in our words and deeds.

It is that vision which lay at the heart of everything we did with the young people. We involved them in the festivities at Easter, Christmas and the holy days of the church. They were times of great cultural diversity, with songs, poems and other contributions. And we taught them that there is no part of the Christian's life that is inadmissible to God, where the claims of God's truth and his justice do not rightfully reign.

And there is a cost in following Christ in this way. Many of our young people discovered this as the

Securitate took an increasing interest in their involvement with the Church and began to make life difficult for them.

The work with young people grew out of that conviction that Christianity and the culture of one's country cannot be separated. The Bible says that when you become a Christian your mind is renewed, and so with that renewing of your mind comes a new view of the world in which you live.

I saw no conflict at all, therefore, between my position as a pastor and my involvement with the Cultural Centre in Dej. This was a focus of the Hungarian community. A limited amount of Hungarian cultural expression was permitted by the authorities: an amateur theatre, folk dancing, concerts and so on. I became involved in the administration of the theatre and organised poetry recitals. Hungarians revere their poets and poetry is as important as music in the heart of a true Hungarian, and so it was in our communities in Transylvania. For me it was a great pleasure to be doing these things, for literature and poetry are things that I love too.

So I was involved with the life of the community in two ways – as a clergyman and as somebody active in the cultural identity of the Hungarian minority. For that, I was constantly attacked. Soon I was allowed only minimal contact with the Cultural Centre on the grounds that I was a 'clerical reactionary'. I was accused of behaviour that was unacceptable to the Party. In Dej, Communism and its atheistic creed dominated the life of the community. A cleric bringing faith and religious perspectives into the common life was intolerable to the authorities. Thus, in a number of different ways, I was pushed out of my work in the Centre.

Having removed my influence from the community at large, they then began a four-year campaign against my work with the young people. It was a constant struggle for me to continue, and a great grief to me. For example, I sometimes discovered my possessions had been moved, and realised that my room had been searched. I was given support by both students and their parents, but the attacks, both verbal and practical, against me continued. The students themselves were also harassed by the Securitate. I had expected opposition from the Securitate and the cultural authorities. What hurt bitterly was the fact that my own bishop would not support me.

Gyula Nagy, Bishop of Transylvania, was not an evil man. He was not made of the stuff of which tyrants and dictators are made. He was fundamentally a weak individual who had early on decided that to struggle against the regime was futile. He was appointed to the bishopric by the Party, and he served his masters well. In later years, locked in struggles with his colleague in Nagyvarad, Bishop Laszlo Papp, I often compared the two. Papp, in my opinion, was a strategist for the regime, actively working against the cause of Christ and the welfare of the Hungarian community in which he was a bishop. Nagy, on the other hand, was a passive, submissive person. He lived during one of the great crises of the Church, and he failed to make a stand. If Papp was the scriptwriter for the drama that resulted in his own overthrow in December 1989, Nagy was much more a creation of the drama itself. He was a playwright written by the play.

In my confrontations with him when I was at Dej, my overriding feeling was one of sorrow. It was a tragedy for me that I could not say to the young people in my church, 'The Securitate harass you, you are persecuted by the State, but look: you have a bishop who will defend you.'

On the contrary, the bishop formally criticised me for doing the very things which the law of the Church prescribed; teaching and training the young, and making the Bible relevant and important to them. It was the obligation of every pastor to do this, but hardly any dared to, except a few who as a result suffered continual harassment and persecution.

In all my activities with the young people I never broke the law. I was not the kind of revolutionary who attempts to topple thrones by the gun and the sword. There was quite enough work to do in simply trying to persuade the Church leaders to operate according to the existing laws of the Church.

Thus, it was forbidden in the Church to invite young people for special instruction. It was a rule initiated by the regime, of course, who understood that young people are the hope and the lifeblood of the Church. So I did not announce the meetings as youth meetings. When I started the Bible hour, I announced it generally and made a point of saying to the students that they were most welcome to come along as well. But such was the hunger of the young people to study God's word that before long they comprised almost the entire membership of the group.

There was another reason for the bishop's displeasure and the increasing attention of the Securitate. It related to the decision that I and my friends had made – that beginning at Brasov we would try to change the condition of the Church in so far as we could. We had no dreams of toppling the regime or of launching a revolution, because the task seemed insuperable. Communism was tightly woven into our society and secured by a complex system of government control and information networks unrivalled anywhere in the world.

We looked at our Church and we saw neglect and failure everywhere. We saw pastors who were weak, frightened, and in some cases openly serving the atheist regime. We saw buildings falling into decay, and resources dwindling as the historic lands and properties of the Church were confiscated and the income from them vanished too. And we thought, as young men just finishing our theological studies, that it ought to be possible to make a change where we were; to plan our careers strategically, look for opportunities to rebuild the Church and challenge the schizophrenia of the age.

For us the Church, despite the corruption and weakness, was a mighty fortress and defence. We took the words of Martin Luther's great hymn and saw in the Church the greatness he ascribed to the city of God. Like Luther, we dreamed of entering that fortress, cleansing it and re-equipping it, and then from behind its walls venturing out against the monolith of the Communist State.

That was what had brought us to Brasov as junior chaplains, and it was the same desire that had motivated me to go to Dej. My strategy was in two parts. First, I decided to work as hard as I possibly could to rebuild the congregational and community spirit and to restore the Bible as the guiding principle of life. I wanted to bring Scripture out of the shadow of the State. That was why I began the Bible group, and why I had been involved in the theatre group for as long as the regime tolerated me.

The second part of my strategy was to challenge the Church leadership directly. I wanted to lobby the bishops, deaneries and pastors. I was young, I was impatient and I was angry.

So at Dej I began to write letters.

One constant problem in the church services was the lack of hymn books and service books. It was one way in which the regime controlled the Church; they made reprinting illegal. Consequently most people treasured their service books until the pages became loose and fell out; then they tied the book up with string and continued to use it.

Bibles, too, were in very short supply. Ceausescu, in the 1970s, was very anxious to be seen in the West as a good ruler, and in many clever ways he managed to give the impression that in Romania religious freedoms were preserved. There is a well-known story that he allowed 10,000 Bibles to be shipped to Romania from the West. But instead of distributing them to the churches, he sent them to a paper mill where they were made into lavatory paper. At the same time, people were being imprisoned in Romania for the crime of smuggling Bibles into the country.

I was scandalised by this situation. What was the Church hierarchy doing about it? Where were the protests to the government, the bishops' objections, the outcry in the congregations? There were none.

So I wrote to every pastor in the diocese asking

how many hymn books and Bibles they had in their church. I wanted evidence to build up a picture of the present state of the Church's resources.

During my years at Dej, I wrote many letters on many subjects. I was fighting a crusade within the Church, and the pen was my strongest weapon. One subject on which I wrote was as follows: Thirty years previously there had been a pastor in one of the Dej village churches. But he had other ambitions. He left the Church and took a State appointment. He remained a State employee for twenty years, paid to further the work of the atheistic regime. Then he decided he wanted to work in the Church again, and Bishop Nagy appointed him head of finance for the diocese. So the man who had been helping to persecute the Church for twenty years was now responsible for deciding how much pastors should be paid, what funds should be available for Christian work in the parish, and all the other financial affairs of the diocese of Transylvania.

It was an outrage. Many people thought so, but nobody did anything about it. So I wrote an open letter deploring this man's turncoat career.

Another open letter I wrote during those years was to Bishop Laszlo Papp, Bishop of Nagyvarad. He had publicly condemned a celebrated Hungarian writer resident in Hungary, Gyula Illyes. He charged Illyes with nationalism and chauvinism – the same charges that had been made by the Securitate against me when they called me in for interview at Brasov. I wrote to Papp arguing that somebody who protected and affirmed the rights of Hungarians in Romania should himself be protected, not denounced, by any bishop of the Hungarian Reformed Church.

Yet another activity in which I was engaged in those years was journalism. Those of us involved were attacking the State's monopoly on information. I began to contribute to a *samizdat* newspaper.

Samizdat began to be an important phenomenon in Eastern Europe in the early 1970s. In countries where the State controlled all the newspapers and broadcast media, there was no opportunity to publish dissenting opinions, and often no opportunity to speak the truth against the State's rhetoric of lies and misinformation. Those who wanted to speak out published their material in secret and distributed it secretly. Thus the underground press flourished.

In *samizdat* writings the voice of believers could be heard, while in the official religious publications only the State-dictated platitudes and propaganda of the official Church spokesmen appeared.

It was an ideal vehicle for those of us who were discontented with the condition of the Church. My first involvement with an underground newspaper was during my time at Dej when a group of friends started the first underground newspaper in the country. It was called *Counterpoints*. It was the brainchild of Karoly Toth, and the work was shared by two others: Attila Ara-Kovacs, and Geza Szocs, who is today a Senator in Romania.

Typewriters were strictly controlled in Romania. The rule was that if you owned one you had to register it with the State. And when you registered it an official came to your office or your home and told you exactly where it was to be located. From time to time inspectors called to check that the typewriter was where it was supposed to be.

Such was the stranglehold Ceausescu's regime

maintained over the means of distributing information. Our newspaper was produced laboriously and imperfectly, using the most rudimentary methods of printing.

In 1981 I began to contribute articles on the state of the Church. We knew that it was only a matter of time before the Securitate discovered the newspaper and its contributors.

My situation became increasingly embattled. The bishop's office had become more and more angry at my frequent outbursts against the bishop, and especially at my claims that the Church was corrupt and guilty of collaboration.

The State, too, was angry at my interference with its puppet diocese. They made my life difficult in many ways. For example, I planned to continue my studies. After the frustration of Kolozsvar Theological Institute, I wanted to explore theology in more depth, to grapple with issues which had been barely touched. So I applied to be admitted to a postgraduate course of study which would have resulted in my gaining a doctorate, following in my father's footsteps. Acceptance or rejection for such courses was firmly in the control of the State. My application was not approved.

In 1983 the Securitate finally discovered *Counterpoints* and punished its editors with great severity. Though I was not directly punished, I knew that I was known to be associated with the newspaper. The Securitate increased their harassment, interfering with my domestic life and causing me trouble in my work.

Matters came to a head in 1984, after the congregation at Dej decided that they needed another

pastor. In congregational elections that year they
passed a formal resolution to create a second pastoral appointment and proceeded to elect me to the
new post. Somewhat surprisingly, the bishop's
office approved their decision.

But after the election the State initiated proceedings against me. The case was actually brought by a
Church disciplinary committee, so nobody knew
that it was a State lawsuit. But the committee was
convened by the disciplinary inspector, the State
employee in charge of Church affairs. The principle
charge was that as a newly ordained minister, I
had sent letters questioning the quality of Church
resources; this meant that I was working against
the Church and against the State itself. It was
also claimed that I had slandered the Church
leaders.

The disciplinary inspector chose the committee
and it was a bizarre collection of people. For example, one man had a son who was an alcoholic,
and there had been a notorious incident in which his
son had actually vomited on the pulpit. The father,
himself an alcoholic, was desperate to do anything
he could to prevent his son being excommunicated
for the offence. The father was a willing puppet in
the hands of the Securitate, and the inspector
brought the son on to the disciplinary committee. It
was men such as he who heard the case, found me
guilty and dismissed me from the ministry.

I immediately appealed to the bishop's office. The
case was heard next by the diocesan court, and it
upheld my appeal, saying that there was insuf-
ficient evidence. So I was reinstated. The whole
process had taken six months. Because the case had
been registered for appeal, the dismissal was never

carried out and I continued my work in the parish throughout.

By now the State authorities were thoroughly annoyed at the failure of the bishop's office to remove me as they wished. Considerable pressure was put upon them to secure the desired result. Having failed to carry through my dismissal once, they tried again. This time they seized on a legal loophole. There had, they said, been a procedural error in the election that had called me as a second pastor.

The document that had been sent to the bishop's office informing them of the election had been improperly drawn up, they said. It was laid down quite clearly that the correct method of presentation was that the decision to create the new pastoral status be set out in one document and a separate document should inform the office which candidate had been elected to that post. The congregational sessions had submitted both the election result and my name as appointee on the same sheet of paper.

Therefore the whole matter was rendered invalid, said the bishop's office in Kolozsvar. Despite the fact that the congregational session had approved my appointment, they received a letter informing them that because of the documentary irregularity, Pastor Tokes could not be their second pastor; he must remain an assistant pastor.

There was a reason for this extraordinary manoeuvring. A full pastor is answerable only to the local congregation, but an assistant pastor is directly responsible to his bishop. It is the bishop who decides where the assistant pastor should work, not the senior pastor with whom he works.

It was no surprise, therefore, that immediately after the letter had been sent another arrived. This stated that as I was now an assistant pastor again, Bishop Nagy was sending me to the tiny village of Uzdiszentpeter, forty kilometres from Kolozsvar. The move was a punishment. Bishop Nagy listed my faults: the work with the young people, the letters I had written, insubordination against the leaders of the Church . . .

I refused to accept the decision of Bishop Nagy, and wrote to tell him so. I pointed out that the activities mentioned in his letter, far from being illegal, were in fact required by the articles of my appointment. I pointed out, too, that it was contrary to Church law for a bishop to overturn a decision taken by a church congregation as to who should be their pastor.

The case attracted a great deal of publicity. Some said that I was unwilling to go to Uzdiszentpeter because it was a small, obscure village and I wanted the limelight. But that was not true. What I objected to was the illegality of Nagy's methods.

I stayed where I was, in the manse in Dej. The bishop's office moved a second time to dismiss me from the ministry. This time the appeal was unsuccessful and the decision was confirmed. I was dismissed, unfrocked, and went home to Kolozsvar, to my parents' house.

During these years my father, too, was speaking out against the government. As a deputy bishop and a professor, he had long been appalled by the condition of the Church. For example, there were seven students in the Theological Institute who were threatened with expulsion. Their offence: they were considered too pious, too religious in their beliefs. My father argued, 'It is a tragedy that the institute should wish to expel students because they are *too religious*.' His campaign on behalf of the students prevented their expulsion.

Another cause he championed was the need for a larger annual intake of students. His well-researched statements to the authorities and regular pleas at Church congresses and college meetings earned him admiration in some quarters and a reputation as a dangerous dissenter in others.

To these two causes, he now added that of his son. He protested that the case had been improperly heard, that basic principles of ecclesiastical law had been ignored; and he defended me articulately with scholarship and with passion.

In 1983 Bishop Gyula Nagy stripped my father of all posts he held in the Church. His dismissal and my own were closely linked. It was generally understood that my father was dismissed for two reasons: as deputy bishop, he stood in the way of the regime's total control of the bishop's office; and he was a bad influence on me and much too good a fighter in my defence.

People sometimes said to me, 'You were dismissed from the Church, you were sentenced by a disciplinary committee and by the bishop. But your father was deputy bishop only a year earlier. Why didn't he use his influence then?'

But my father was dismissed precisely because of the stand he took in support of his son. He risked his livelihood and his calling in order to make an unpopular stand. It was one more example of that seamless integration of faith and life that had been instilled in me from my earliest childhood.

4

THE YEARS OF WAITING

With my father and myself at home and very little money coming into the house, life was very hard for my mother. Even my father's literary skills could not produce a reasonable income.

To mask the possible scandal of a deputy bishop's being forcibly removed from his post, he was given a rare permission to publish his books. He was the only minister writing theological works in the diocese, so they allowed him to publish. The condition they imposed upon him was that he was forbidden to earn more than 11,000 lei (about £300) for each book. The typewriting costs alone accounted for 5,000 lei, so the books made little contribution to the family budget.

Yet it was a concession. My father, who was working on a book on hermeneutics at the time, said, 'I don't want the money; I just want my book to get into the hands of my brother pastors and theologians.' To deflect any criticism from the public of the derisory payment my father received for his work, the state allowed him to publish one book every year.

I enjoyed being back in family life. I had lived a

solitary, almost monastic, existence for several years now. When asked whether I intended to marry, I would say half humorously that I was like a Catholic priest, devoted only to the cause of the Church. Though it was meant as a joke, there was more than a grain of truth in it. My attitude to marriage had always been one of near-celibacy; as a young man I had been revolted at the thought of acquiescing in the virtual arranged marriages of the collaborating pastors' 'dynastic' families, and when I was an adult I was too involved with my work to consider marriage. I used to think of myself as wedded to the Church, not in a mystical way but simply because the Church and the struggles that I and my friends were engaged in consumed all our energies and passions.

However, marriage was not something I repudiated. Often, seeing Christian marriages in the community in which I worked, or remembering the happy marriage of my parents and the loving atmosphere in which I grew up, I recognised that a Christian wife and a Christian home were among the greatest gifts that God could give a pastor.

I had known Edit since I first arrived in Dej and we had become close friends. She was born in Dej where she still lived, and so had been brought up in the same part of Romania as I had. I had often met her as I travelled round the deanery. Our friendship had deepened, and as a result she too had suffered harassment by the Securitate. In 1985, after I had been expelled from the Dej pastorship and prohibited from taking further office in the Church, life was much less busy, and we realised that our friendship had become something much deeper. We decided to marry.

There was an irony in the timing of our wedding. The winter of 1984–5 had been devastating. In the bitter cold there was little heat and light. Fuel shortages meant that power supplies were often cut off and heating in public places was hardly permitted at all. In sub-zero temperatures, many old people and babies died. Ceausescu ordered hospitals to switch off incubators in maternity departments, and patients dependent on life-support systems also lost their lives. Most of the population spent their days and nights in one room of their homes, huddled together to conserve what little heat there was.

It was in that period, paradoxically, that Ceausescu initiated his humiliating and inhuman crusade to raise the population level. All married women were ordered to produce four children each or be punished by severe taxes. Pregnant women were examined each month to make sure that there was no abortion attempt. Despite this, the number of illegal abortions increased dramatically: women did not want to bring babies into a world as bleak as Ceausescu's Romania. But legal abortion was not available and contraception was illegal. The results of thousands of appallingly badly managed back-street abortions have horrified the West since photographers were first allowed into the Romanian orphanages following the Revolution. We in Romania were horrified too, for no member of the public was ever allowed into an orphanage during Ceausescu's reign.

So it was a very strange time to be marrying. The economy was increasingly bleak, the future for children born in Romania was grimmer than ever before, and I had just experienced a devastating blow to all my hopes and expectations for the future. And yet we decided to marry. We loved each other, and it was a symbol of hope.

One of the Old Testament prophets, Jeremiah, was imprisoned and opposed, and he bought land in Judah, knowing that the country was doomed to be overthrown. No doubt everybody laughed at him. 'How can you buy land now, when you have no hope for the future?' We wanted our marriage to reflect that degree of hope. Although we knew the seriousness of the situation and understood the tragic destiny towards which Ceausescu had launched his country, we did not accept it fatalistically. We had a hope that one day things would be better.

Our wedding was a major local event. We invited all the people from the church. It was a festival, for the church had supported me during all the struggles of the past few years. They had repudiated the acts of Bishop Nagy and the regime. There were about three hundred guests at the wedding and at the reception afterwards. We invited friends from all over Transylvania.

Of course, the Securitate found it all extremely interesting. They took photographs at the wedding and reception, made notes during the speeches, and when during the day there was a spontaneous and controlled demonstration, they filmed that as well. Their base was a room in the hotel in which the reception was held and they monitored everything with calculated efficiency. After the wedding, many of our guests were summoned to the Securitate offices and questioned.

Edit was a teacher and had to work away from Dej. Like many Romanian couples, we were separated by work requirements for twelve months after our marriage. It was part of Ceausescu's forced assimilation policy.

As I think of the two years I spent exiled from the ministry, three quotations very important to us at that time come to mind. In the Heidelberg Confession there is a promise that God makes good even what is bad provided we trust in Him. In the eighth chapter of his letter to the Romans, the apostle Paul writes, 'We know that in all things God works for the good of those who love Him.' And in the Old Testament, at the end of the book of Genesis, Joseph points out that though his brothers tried to do evil against him, God turned it into good.

As I took stock of my situation after the trauma of the expulsion, I became more determined than ever to fight against the regime. I resolved to find the best methods to use against it. My main activity was as a campaigner for human rights in the context of church life.

I must have written several kilos' worth of letters, protesting at the injustice that had been done to me. I wrote to every forum of discussion in the country, I wrote to the church and also to the Communist Party. I even wrote to Ceausescu. He did not reply. In fact, very few people at all replied.

At that point I could have abandoned my efforts and accepted that my church career was at an end. But instead I redoubled my efforts. Edit and I were living in Kolozsvar in my parents' home; every night I saw my father working at his desk on my behalf, studying volumes of Church law, constructing a case that might convince the authorities that what had been done to me was illegal in the law of the Church. His example inspired me to return to the attack.

In my letters I informed the recipients that I intended to demonstrate in some way against my punishment. Every day I donned my black vestments and went to the bishop's palace in Kolozsvar where I sat from 8 a.m. to 4 p.m. in the courtyard. When people asked me what I was doing, I replied: 'I am a minister in the Hungarian Reformed Church who has no church to pastor. Isn't that strange? And we thought our Church was in great need of pastors . . .'

And sometimes I made even more elaborate protests, such as the time I attended a big theological conference being held at the institute. I attended every lecture, a conspicuous six-footer dressed in formal clerical suit. When the opportunity came for delegates to ask questions, twice I tried to make a statement, though I was prevented each time. One of the speakers, an adviser from the bishop's office named Karoly Szekely, warned me that I would be in trouble if I persisted. So I tried again, this time in a full session of the conference when he was speaking.

Szekely glared at me and addressed the audience. 'Do not worry, I have warned Mr Tokes and now, if he does not immediately sit down, the police will be called. Will somebody please remove him from the conference?'

He was trying to create a mood of hostility in the hall, so that soon everybody would be shouting, 'Make Laszlo Tokes leave!' But when he announced that he would call the police, there was only silence.

The reactions of friends and colleagues to my actions during this period varied. From my parents I received only unqualified support. Edit was a strength and comfort. I had once remarked that when I considered all that my father had achieved, all that he managed to do for the cause of Christ and for his fellow human beings, it was only when I looked at my mother's tireless and sacrificial labours that I realised how it was possible. Now Edit joined me in the struggle in countless ways.

Others were mixed in their attitude. I visited the Theological Institute and talked with one of the professors, Tamas Juhasz. Sitting in the quiet of his apartment, in a friendly room crammed with books and pictures, its windows looking out on to the peaceful quiet of the courtyard, we discussed my situation.

'I have to confess I think you made the wrong decision,' he said.

'What do you think I ought to have done?' I replied.

'Maybe you should have accepted the injustice. Maybe you should have agreed to the bishop's decision to move you to the tiny village. Then after a year, or even half a year, if you kept quiet and didn't make any more criticisms, the bishop would have forgotten all about Laszlo Tokes. The Securitate would have thought they had defeated you.'

'What would that have achieved?'

'Then in time you would have been elected to a full pastorship in the city. Then the bishop wouldn't have had the power to dictate to you and you would have been where you wanted to be.'

'I wanted to be at Dej,' I said.

Through the window I could see the institute

buildings, drab and badly in need of repair. The courtyard, through which generations of students had passed, could have done with a spring-clean. What was once a jewel in the Reformed Church had lost its lustre. Like our churches and our manses, the institute was being drained of essential funds, kept on a deliberately low budget by a hostile regime.

'People have been silent under injustice for too long,' I said abruptly.

The situation in the country after the terrible winter was made much worse by Ceausescu's policies. All farmland had been owned by the State since 1974 and food production rigorously controlled. Now Ceausescu decided to eradicate Romania's national debt. His method was to strip the country of its resources and sell them abroad.

The results created a nightmare social order. Industrial complexes with minimal or non-existent public health safeguards poured out produce and pollution. In towns like Copsa Mica not far from Kolozsvar, the fields, houses, animals and the people themselves were black with soot from the local factory. Having raped the industrial resources of Romania – one of the richest countries in mineral wealth in Europe – the dictator abused farmland. Overfertilised season after season, the fields were never allowed to lie fallow and regain their goodness. The crops were gathered remorselessly, but the plants were stunted and the fruit was of increasingly poor quality.

Almost all the country's produce was exported and the people queued miserably for what was left.

In 1985, the hardship and suffering of the people

brought a good deal of Western attention to Romania. Previously, Romania's reputation abroad had been coloured by Ceausescu's initial nonalignment with Moscow and his denunciation (later retracted) of the Soviet invasion of Czechoslovakia in 1968. He also had one of the most tolerant attitudes in Eastern Europe to the Jewish community, a factor that helped Romania gain Most Favoured Nation status with America. In Britain, Ceausescu was made Knight Grand Cross of the Order of the Bath. The insignia were given pride of place in the History Museum in Bucharest along with his Légion d'Honneur and a display drawing attention to his honorary citizenship of Disneyland, USA.

In the West, he was seen as a solitary bastion against the Moscow caucus. But there had been deep concern over human rights issues, for example following the revelations of Pastor Richard Wurmbrand about prison conditions and religious persecution in the country, and Pastor Josef Tson's challenge to the socialist leadership following his contacts with students at Oxford at the end of the 1960s. In the mid-1970s Karoly Kiraly, a member of the Central Committee of the Party, spoke out against the treatment of Hungarian minorities in Romania. For this he was placed under house arrest, and ended up running a small factory in Tirgu-Mures. Pressure from the West resulted in the freeing of almost all religious prisoners by 1986.

Now the West was again concerned, this time over the hardships of the people, and the subject of Romania began to occur frequently in the Western media. The events that were to bring us into the forefront of human rights stories still lay in the future. But there had been a grim foreshadowing when, in 1984, Ceausescu began to destroy the heart of the capital, Bucharest, one of the great cities of Europe, in order to create a socialist palace and boulevard. Churches, historic buildings and monuments and streets that had remained essentially unchanged for centuries were swept away to make the grandiose dream a reality.

This vision of megalomania was to develop in ways that few of us could have dreamed of.

As Romania slid deeper into its troubles, I and my friends increased our efforts. The demise of *Counterpoints* had simply redoubled our attempts to be heard. Geza Szocs, the editor, had been expelled from Romania; today he is secretary of the Democratic Alliance of Hungarians in Romania. Those of us who remained had to continue the work.

I wrote several articles for theological journals, discussing the failures of the Church adequately to oppose what was happening both on the national and the ecclesiastical level. I also took every opportunity to follow the same cultural interests that I had pursued in Dej.

Our *samizdat* activities had been an attempt to stand against the State. The events in Dej and the harassment by the Securitate had only made me more radical in my ambitions.

What had happened to me was a symptom of the collapse of Church integrity and collaboration between the Church and the atheistic State. I was unemployed, thrown out of the Church, but God had given me a task – not to mourn my own plight and fight for my reinstatement, but to fight for a resolution of the problem of the Church.

I and my friends realised that if we were going to

achieve substantial results, we would have to do even more than we had done so far. During 1985 we launched a major letter-writing campaign. We took the names and addresses from the telephone book, choosing people with Hungarian names from all over Transylvania; we had no guarantee that they really were Hungarians, but it was very likely.

We appealed to them to maintain what Hungarian education facilities remained. We pointed out that Ceausescu's policy was to disperse forcibly the Hungarian population, and that the implications for all minorities and for Romania itself were disastrous.

There were already many examples of the regime's treatment of other denominations to warn us that the State was fundamentally opposed to religious freedom. The truth could not be hidden any longer despite the official lies and the cynicism that led to privileges being granted to religious groups to serve the purpose of the State. (The Orthodox Church, for example, with a predominantly ethnic Romanian membership, was given many freedoms.)

Producing the letters was a slow, laborious process. We had no access to photocopiers and typewriters were strictly controlled. We had to resort to writing by hand and producing photographs with a camera. The cost was enormous – we produced 12,000 letters – but we were able to raise the money from donations by friends. Then we took the letters all over Romania and posted them from Bucharest, Craiova and several other cities, to make sure they could not be traced back to us.

We made use of the time in the various cities outside Transylvania to compile statistics: for ex-

ample, the number of Hungarians studying at the
universities and what percentage they formed of the
total number of students.

This was a very necessary exercise to gain
ammunition for our cause. We were concerned
about government discrimination. The reason for
numbers declining at Kolozsvar Theological Institute was the limitation on entrants by the State. No
statistics relating to minorities were available. Very
few statistics of any kind were published by the
government and access to reliable data was virtually
impossible.

It might be claimed, for example, that twenty per
cent of students at Kolozsvar University were ethnic
Hungarians, and it might then be argued that this
was an adequate figure for a minority community.
But there were now Hungarians all over Romania,
and the Kolozsvar figure looked very different, if,
for example, it could be demonstrated that at
Bucharest University the percentage of Hungarian
students was only half of one per cent.

Indeed, we would have been glad if even the State
limitations were observed; for the reality was that
the State rarely met its own targets. We almost
envied people like the South African black community. At least they knew what their options were.
They knew what was permitted and what was
forbidden. In Romania everything was confused.

We were assured that we had religious freedom.
Our own colleagues, our bishops and most of the
clergy said they were satisfied this was true. It was a
wall of lies. And we set out to make a breach in it.

I was well aware that every honest Christian agreed
with me in my analysis of the problem. Where

people differed was in their attitudes to it. And different attitudes produce different consequences. Some people faced with an obstacle see no alternative but to remove it. Others come to a standstill in front of it. Others still go under it and continue on their way. There are so many attitudes, so many possible courses of action.

A typical attitude was that of the conformist, the person who submits to the demands of the regime and practises his or her faith only in so far as the demands of the atheistic state permit. And even the compromisers and conformers knew in their hearts what the truth of the situation was. Somewhere in their hearts they knew that we were right. Not all conformists were corrupted like the bishops. Many just wanted to survive, and the only way they knew was by conforming.

Between the conformist attitude and the attitude of those who were activists for change there was a great difference. The conformist had made a basic concession to history. He had conceded that the situation could not be changed, and so he changed himself to fit in with it. We who campaigned did so not in order to change ourselves in a negative way, but to change the situation in a positive way. It was a guiding principle in everything we did.

This was our revolutionary ideal; not a revolution of the barricades, but a revolutionary perspective. And, of course, a revolution of the mind, for without changing one's way of thinking one can never arrive at this point.

I was unemployed for two years. I was not the only Christian minister to be persecuted by the regime. Many others from many denominations suffered

during those years, many far worse than I did. The
case of Father Calciu, for example, was well known
in the West. He was a member of the Lord's Army,
a proscribed movement within the Orthodox
Church. In 1973, ten years after completing a
sixteen-year prison sentence in the notorious Pitesti
Prison, he was made professor of New Testament
theology in Bucharest. His influence among the
young was enormous. In 1979 he spoke out against
Ceausescu's destruction of churches. He was
arrested and treated with appalling brutality, then
sentenced to ten years in prison. In 1984 he was
released, but the Securitate ordered him to be de-
frocked. Eventually, his ministry in ruins, he was
allowed to leave Romania. Those in the West who
thought that the atrocities endured by people such
as Richard Wurmbrand had disappeared in the
early 1980s were horrified when his story became
known. The list of those who have suffered for
Christ in Romania is a long one and crosses all
boundaries of nationality and denomination.

It is striking that most of those who have been
persecuted in Romania have said that pressure from
the West made a considerable difference to the way
they were treated. Ceausescu himself was expert at
orchestrating his public clemency to coincide with
the annual Most Favoured Nation status review in
which the special relationship with America was
confirmed. Calciu himself was released just before a
review and allowed to emigrate just before another.

In my case, many friends from the West voiced
their concern about my unjust dismissal from Dej.
American politicians gave my case publicity, including the foreign secretary, who personally made an
appeal against my defrocking when he visited

Romania in 1985. Christian organisations gave us encouragement. Keston College, the information centre in Britain that monitors religious freedoms in Eastern Europe, supported us in many ways. There were many, many people who showed concern for the situation in Romania, and we were grateful to every one of them.

The pressure from outside, the regime's desire for good relations with the West and the pressure exerted by the campaigning of myself and my friends brought a crisis upon the authorities in Kolozsvar. Either I must be done away with like a number of dissidents who had been involved in inexplicable car accidents or strange sudden deaths, or they would have to take away my main platform – the charge of unjust dismissal – in an attempt to weaken my case.

It appears that they chose the latter option, for in 1986 a review committee finally reconsidered my case and reinstated me as an ordained minister in the Hungarian Reformed Church. Shortly afterwards I was invited by Laszlo Papp, the Bishop of Nagyvarad, to take the post of assistant pastor in the Hungarian Reformed Church in Temesvar.

The strategy was clear. Temesvar was a town far away from Kolozsvar and my friends. An assistant pastor could be controlled directly by the bishop. The appointment was a clever way of burying me in obscurity.

So they sent me to Temesvar, little knowing that three years later it would become – for a few days – the most famous city in the world.

5

TEMESVAR – A CHURCH COMES ALIVE

The politics underlying my appointment to Temes-var were complex. There were conflicts of which I became only gradually aware.

Leo Peuker was the pastor whom I was to assist. Born a Jew, he converted to Catholicism and became a Roman Catholic priest. Four or five years later he met the woman whom he was later to marry and changed religion again, joining the Reformed Church. When I knew him, he often spoke of the high regard in which he was held by the Orthodox community, and I believe that if he had been given an extra life, he would in due course have converted to the Orthodox priesthood.

In the 1960s he ran against Laszlo Papp in the election for the bishopric of Nagyvarad. Both were informers for the Securitate, both were widely known as collaborators with the regime and both wanted to be bishop and benefit from the privileges that went with the job. Papp won, and Peuker was a bad loser. The two were now enemies.

Sending me to Temesvar was a clever move. The bishop, wanting to make sure his rival was safely out of the way, saddled him with a known dissident

Above: A typical Transylvanian landscape in the hills near Kolozsvar.

Left: From January 1990 I began to receive speaking invitations from all over the world.

Above: The Opera Square, Temesvar. The numbers of those who died here in the December massacre will probably never be known.

Below: My friend, Lajos Varga, outside my apartment in the church building, Temesvar. During the day on December 15th 1989, I spoke to the crowd from this window and food and other gifts were passed to us.

Looking from my study through the same window. From the building opposite, Securitate spies watched our movements during 1989 and probably earlier.

Above: The manse, Mineu. This building became a fortified prison for a few days after our forced removal from Temesvar.

Below: Mineu seems much farther from its nearest town than it actually is; its isolation is emphasised by the primitive roads and tracks that lead there.

Mineu

Above: 'Long live Laszlo Tokes', painted by our supporters on the church wall in Temesvar. An election poster below shows me as a candidate for the Democratic Alliance of Hungarians in the May 1990 elections.

Below: In Budapest Stadium in February 1990 I addressed a large audience of Hungarians and Romanians. I spoke in both languages and artistes from both communities performed.

Above: My father and mother, Istvan and Erzsebet Tokes.

Below: Edit and I with Mate.

A family group in 1958. Reading from left to right: Myself, Andras, Anna, Istvan, Erzsebet, Eszter, Jozsef. Between my mother and father: Zsolt.

Above: The choir, Szepkenyeruszentmarton, c.1975.

Below: After the revolution, such was the feeling against Laszlo Papp in Nagyvar that most of the photographs and records of him were destroyed. This is one of few photographs that remain in the church archives, of which only a photocopy available.

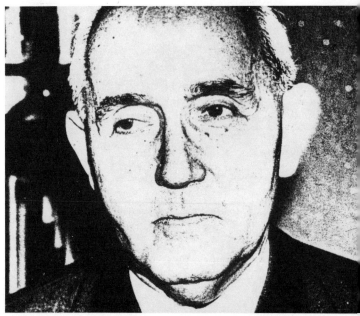

as a partner. Peuker would be guilty by association; some of my notoriety would rub off on him, reasoned Papp, and keeping me under control would distract Peuker from his own ambitions.

On the other hand, Peuker was a spy and Papp wanted me watched. So I was to be under Peuker's surveillance. He reported from day to day and week to week on all my activities: what I had been doing, who I had been talking to, what I had said. Thus the bishop achieved two objectives.

It was a kind of ecclesiastical exile. Temesvar, almost on the Yugoslav border, was distant from Kolozsvar and Dej in which Edit and I had grown up.

Built in the earliest years of the medieval Hungarian kingdom, it was for some time the capital of Hungary. Great names in our history are associated with the city: King Matthias and his father, Janos Hunyadi, whose heroism in 1456 prevented the Turks from occupying Hungary. But in 1552 Temesvar was besieged by the Turks who ruled it until 1716, when it was retaken by Habsburg-Hungarian troops. During the eighteenth century the Habsburg Catholics refused to allow Hungarian Protestants to settle in Temesvar. Not until the nineteenth century were Protestants permitted residence in the city.

So unlike Dej, where the Hungarian Reformed Church was the main historic Church with roots going back uninterruptedly to the fourteenth century, Temesvar was a city whose history was bisected. There are no historic links with the Reformation. The defeat of the Turks in 1716 involved the destruction of all the churches and of the city itself. Today you cannot find a building in Temesvar that is older than the eighteenth century.

Temesvar is now, through the ravages of history, on the perimeter of Hungarian Transylvania. It is a predominantly Romanian city with a minority Hungarian population. When we arrived, there were only 10,000 Hungarian Protestants in a total population of 400,000.

I arrived in June 1986. Temesvar is a city with a fine centre: the Bega Canal runs through it, and there are parks and pleasant tree-lined avenues still preserving something of the graceful plan of the Hungarian who built the city and christened it Temesvar. Today the centre is drab and neglected, and outside it are acres of bleak apartment blocks, badly built constructions planted in wastelands of rubble and stagnant, weedy puddles. The Hungarian Church is in the centre, on the second floor of an apartment block that would not be out of place in London, Paris or Vienna. But few of the congregation lived in the centre of the city. That was where the Securitate and Party hierarchy lived.

Our congregation travelled to worship on the clattering trams that crisscrossed Temesvar. It was a journey they only had to make once a week. Under Peuker, the life of the church had dwindled like its congregation. Christianity was reduced to forms and rituals, services were reduced to a bare minimum. There was one service of worship each week, on Sundays, and when necessary burials were conducted. None of the services that were part of the normal life of Reformed Churches were held at all. There was no catechism, no confirmation class, and no Bible group.

Pastor Peuker and pastors like him were ambassadors for the Communist regime. They were given their posts so that they could preach what was not true. Their ministry involved none of the activities that biblical pastors had always considered essential. How could it? They did not have the vision of a true pastor, a shepherd of the people of God. They were in business to promote a different gospel. Peuker himself was an ultraloyalist. He had even preached in his pulpit wearing the red star of Communism on his clerical vestments. He was one of five or six pastors whose reputation for total collaboration had spread throughout the Hungarian Reformed Church. They were known as red priests.

In Temesvar, the effect on the congregation was predictable. Marginalised by a hostile government, spiritually alienated by an uncaring pastor, they lost interest in the church, until fewer than fifty worshippers appeared each Sunday to hear Peuker's moralising homilies.

We arrived in Temesvar with mixed feelings. After two years of frustration at least I now had a job again. And we would have a home. On the other hand, we knew something of Peuker's reputation. How would I be able to withstand the pressures that would undoubtedly be put on me by working so closely with a collaborating pastor?

The reality surpassed our gloomiest fears.

It took a very short time for me to realise that my new 'job' was no job at all. Peuker made it clear that he did not intend to allow me to carry out any of the duties that an assistant pastor would be expected to do. I would not be expected to conduct weddings, baptise children or officiate at burials. Occasionally I was to be allowed to preach, but it would be infrequently. When I appeared in the church office, hoping to be given some task to do, I was ushered out again.

I tried to keep up my theological reading and to occupy myself in various ways, but I was accountable to nobody. I was given no programme. I could do what I liked but there was nothing to do.

I attempted to visit my new parishioners, but everywhere found suspicion and embarrassment. After I had been in Temesvar for a few weeks one or two of them began to talk to me, fearfully and always in secret. Conversations of any depth were impossible.

Our first days in Temesvar were full of loneliness and frustration, made no less so by the fact that Edit was now expecting our first child.

'This,' said Peuker, 'will be your room.'

We looked in disbelief. The room adjoining the main church hall had clearly never been intended for living accommodation. It was small, uncomfortable and separated from the church by a single door. Edit looked round in bewilderment. 'There is no bathroom,' she said hesitantly. 'No lavatory, no fireplace . . .'

'There is an excellent bathroom downstairs, next to the office,' the pastor explained.

We contemplated the bare walls and wondered how we would manage without a fireplace when winter came.

Later I challenged him about the accommodation he had given us.

'The church owns this entire block of apartments,' I pointed out. 'Several of them are empty. Why can't we have one of the empty ones instead of our tiny room?'

Peuker managed to look inflexible and sympathetic at the same time. 'You see, it's not worth it to fix up a whole apartment. It would be a waste of time for you.'

'I don't see why. Our baby is due in September.'

'But by September you may be gone from here. Temesvar is a bad parish,' he said sadly. 'They have no love for pastors here. You must have noticed the attitude of the people when you speak to them. In a few weeks you'll probably decide to move on.'

But by the time September came, we had made our first real friends in Temesvar. Though the small congregation was afraid of Peuker and his links with the Securitate, most of them were outraged at the way we were being treated and the appalling accommodation we had been given. Edit received many small kindnesses and the people made their concern known in ways that we understood and appreciated. One of the congregation, a neighbour from one of the church apartments, introduced himself to us as Jozsef Kabai, and he and his family quickly became close friends. Jozsef's uncompromising honesty and Christian goodness made him despise Peuker's world of deception and half-truths, and he and his family risked persecution from the church authorities as they befriended us from the time we first arrived.

It was from Jozsef Kabai that I learned some of the reasons for our unhappy experiences so far. 'Peuker warned us about you before you arrived,' he said. 'He told us that Mr Tokes was coming and that we must be very wary of you. He said you were a rebel, an enemy of the State. If we associated with you it could be harmful to us.'

'So I arrived already compromised,' I said bitterly. 'An evil reputation all ready and waiting for me.'

'I'll tell you something else,' added Kabai. 'If you look carefully, you'll see the same cars always parked at the end of the street. They're Securitate cars. They've been watching the building ever since you arrived.'

'Laszlo Papp,' I breathed.

'And one more thing,' he added. 'The apartments in the house opposite. Facing Peuker's study. They're a known Securitate base.'

In September Mate was born. Our joy at being given a beautiful healthy child was mixed with frustration at the conditions in which Peuker expected us to care for him. Soon our small room was perpetually full of baby clothes. We had to do all our washing in that room, with water carried up from the bathroom below, and dry Mate's nappies as best we could on makeshift clotheslines strung across the room.

In December my patience ran out. Peuker had admired the baby and said suitable pastoral words, but there had been no hint at all that our domestic needs were being reconsidered. I decided to take more drastic action, and composed a petition to the church presbytery.

I pointed out that our situation was now impossible. Winter had come, the cold penetrating into every corner of the building. We had no firewood. We did not even have a fireplace. When I had raised the matter with Pastor Peuker, he had told me I would have to pay if I wanted a fireplace to be installed. My baby would become ill if something were not done immediately, I said. There was an empty apartment downstairs; I wished the presbytery to authorise our move into it.

I sent the petition and waited to see what the result would be. A few days later Peuker summoned me to his office. He was furious.

'I have had a request from the presbytery,' he stormed. 'Your behaviour in this matter is intolerable.'

He raged on bitterly. 'You have to learn that if you aren't capable of following the directions you have been given, you'll simply make more and more problems for yourself. You were in trouble when you came here. Now you are trying to make more trouble.' His eyes glowed dangerously. 'I should warn you. I have friends who are extremely close to Mr Ceausescu. Let that be a warning to you.'

He calmed down somewhat. He tapped the paper on his desk. 'I shall inform the presbytery that your request is refused.'

Afterwards, I realised that his grotesque anger was probably the result of paranoia. He knew that Bishop Papp had sent me to Temesvar in the hope that I would be a useful spy on his own activities.

But nothing had changed in my situation.

By Christmas, matters had become critical. Edit was struggling more and more, as Mate's needs grew and our room became increasingly cramped and difficult to manage. I was still without meaningful duties, and the approaching festival offered no possibility that things would change. In Christmas week there was a service every day, but Peuker insisted on conducting them all. There were also a great many funerals that month, and he conducted them too; there was a fee payable for burials, and Peuker was greedy.

The congregation were appalled by what was going on, but were powerless to do anything. The enormity of our treatment, however, was brought home to everybody during one of the Christmas week services.

Peuker was in the pulpit. His text was from the second chapter of Luke: 'She wrapped him in strips of cloth and placed him in a manger, because there was no room for them in the inn.' The pastor described at length the child of Bethlehem, forced to sleep among the animals because he had no home.

As his voice droned on, the congregation were distracted by another sound: from behind the door that separated our tiny room from the church, the thin wailing of our baby's crying filled the church.

The workload that Peuker had taken on over Christmas was visibly taking its toll. At the end of each day he was grey with exhaustion, but he did not offer to share the work with me.

On December 27th he was conducting a burial at the cemetery when he collapsed with a heart attack. He was rushed to the hospital where he survived for ten days.

His death was widely regarded in the parish as the hand of God. Peuker, in 1960, had been responsible for the dismissal of his predecessor in Temesvar, an exemplary minister beloved by the community. He was a Hungarian who loved the Hungarian culture and the reformed faith and was a very good pastor to his flock. Thirty years before, as the regime was strengthening its grip on Romania, Peuker worked with the authorities to get rid of him. In the opinion of many local people with whom I talked, Peuker's sins had now come home to roost.

There was no antisemitic flavour to the people's dislike of Leo Peuker. Nor had he suppressed Hungarian culture in his church. Indeed, his own mother had been a Hungarian. As a man, he had once been a colourful personality with a wide circle of friends; a witty conversationalist, contributing intelligently to discussions, and very clever. He read widely, had an encyclopaedic fund of knowledge and a genuine breadth in his view of the world.

He was a true cosmopolitan, a man who was adaptable to any circumstances in which he might find himself. The tragedy was that this was true of his faith too. In a sense he had no nation and no God. He remained neutral. By the time I knew him, he had become a prisoner of his own role, his vitality and enquiring mind stifled by the demands of the regime. The path to the bishop's palace had been denied him; his development as a human being and a spiritual identity was likewise stunted long ago.

Bishop Papp summoned me to his office.

'I am appointing you as a supply pastor in the church at Temesvar,' he said. 'It is a probationary post.' I thought of the long months of doing nothing, of running errands for Peuker and trying to devise ways of occupying my time. How long did I need to prove myself? I had been a full pastor in Dej. The bishop was painting rosy pictures of a successful future. 'From this, you could go very far. Your appointment as full pastor will be confirmed if all goes well.' His tone became sharper. 'It all depends on how you conduct yourself,' he said. 'I am sure you will be a faithful and satisfactory probationer. And then you will be installed as pastor of your church.' He looked at me to make sure I understood what he was saying. 'Otherwise, you will be dismissed.'

I received my articles of appointment as provisory pastor. One of Bishop Papp's advisers was fulsome. 'Really, you could go as far as you want to now that you have this appointment,' he said warmly. 'You could become a dean. You could even become a bishop . . .' Provided, he took pains to emphasise, that I conformed, that I was obedient to my superiors, that I behaved myself.

The strategy of the authorities was very clear to me. In Dej, the Bishop of Kolozsvar and the Securitate had tried by persecution and harassment to force me to conform. Now Bishop Papp and his Securitate colleagues were trying the other way. By dangling promises of ecclesiastical preferment and a glittering future, they hoped to persuade me to obey Papp's orders and cease to be a problem to them.

My appointment had other advantages for them too. Temesvar is a large city near the border, and had the attention of the West. The authorities had not forgotten the intervention on my behalf of the American foreign secretary in 1985. Now America could be told how little substance there was in their fears. Mr Tokes was doing very well; he was pastor of a large city church; he had nothing to complain about any more.

When I took up my new duties in January 1987, the congregation was in complete disarray. We had only 2,500 on the church roll, and very few indeed actually worshipped in the church each Sunday. There was no momentum; the church was slowly grinding to a halt. There was no point in planning great enterprises for the future. Even if I had wanted to, it would have been a waste of energy proposing elaborate church growth programmes or major evangelistic campaigns. We were starting too far back for that. In reality, so bankrupt was our church in every way, we had to start at the very beginning.

My first priority was a thorough stocktaking of the whole of our church life. We needed to gather our flock together, to make sure that we knew each person in the church. Then, having gathered them, our task was to motivate them as a church congregation into becoming a caring, supportive and ministering fellowship. This was our priority not only because of the disastrous policies of Pastor Peuker, but also because we were a minority, reduced in size and struggling for survival in the face of a regime bent on scattering us over the whole land of Romania.

Everything in the church had been run down. Years of neglect had left the church building and furnishings in a very bad state. There were no catechisms for the handful of young people who attended church; Bible instruction and careful, systematic teaching of the young had not figured at all in my predecessor's priorities. Since our arrival the previous summer, I had often longed for the opportunity to work with young people as I had at Dej. Now it had come.

As Edit and I looked at the task that lay ahead of us, we were both apprehensive and excited. The immensity of the task was daunting, but we knew that though the regime and the bishops had intended me to finish my career in obscurity in Temesvar, God had brought us there.

There is a verse from the Old Testament which I have already referred to; it has been relevant at many stages in my life. It comes at the end of the book of Genesis, where it is written that Joseph's brothers, because they were jealous of him, sold him as a slave and watched him carried off to a foreign land. Years later, Joseph had become immensely rich and powerful, raised by the hand of God from the wretchedness of slavery to the highest courts of Egypt. The family was reunited, and there is a moving description of Joseph's reunion with his father, Jacob. But Jacob died, and Joseph's brothers became afraid that he would now seek revenge on them.

But Joseph disarmed their fears with words which I have never forgotten: 'You intended to harm me, but God intended it for good.'

And such was the case in Temesvar, for Bishop Papp's plotting brought us to a place where for the first time I was in charge of a parish. In Brasov I was only a chaplain, and in Dej I had been answerable to a dean. The dean was a good man, but he had been in charge of my activities. Even though I was a full pastor, he was the senior pastor. Now I was on my own, the pastor of a widespread parish in a large city where thousands of people were out of contact with the church. At Temesvar we made deep friendships, saw the hand of God mightily at work in people's lives, and, in the events of December 1989, saw his power overturning empires and overcoming the powers of darkness.

All of which lay far in the future, as we set about the task of rebuilding the church in Temesvar.

The Hungarian Reformed Church is a church of the people. It integrates the church and the community. It has no equivalent among the churches often found in the West, where worship and the life of the church are a 'Sunday' compartment in the lives of the people that does not impinge on their everyday existence at all.

In Temesvar, the church had lost that vision. Seventy per cent of the Hungarian community were not members of the church and had no contact with the reformed faith. So I took the city as a mission field. In my mind it was a mission like that of the apostle Paul, for the secularising influence of the atheistic regime had bitten deep into the hearts of the people.

The presbytery, or team of elders, was weak after years of Peuker's intimidation. I was not the only person he had threatened by claiming relations with the Ceausescu family.

'We have just come to the end of a thirty-year phase in the history of our church in Temesvar,' I told them. 'Now we can start a new phase. But to do that we need the help of every member of presbytery and every parishioner. It is not a matter of my being in charge. I am not the only pastor here; we must all be pastors to each other.'

I was determined not to do what Bishop Papp hoped – to allow myself quietly to settle into the same comfortable rut as Peuker. In all my attitudes to the authorities, both episcopal and secular, I resolved that I would not choose my actions simply as a reaction to their demands. I was going to take the initiative, thus throwing back on them the task of deciding how to react to what *I* was doing.

I was determined to do this because in the

Romanian Constitution the rights and freedoms of religion were guaranteed. That is what the letter of the law said. The fact that it had been so poorly observed under Ceausescu's tyranny changed nothing. Although much of what we did in Temesvar in the early days outraged the authorities, we did nothing that was not legal and prescribed. Just as in Dej, I was never an anarchist. All I wanted to do was to implement the laws of my country and my church.

So we reorganised. Soon catechisms were restored to the life of the church. Young people were prepared for confirmation. New services of worship were held, not only on Sundays. At the great festivals of the Church calendar we held special activities and services of celebration.

In my office we discovered the old baptismal registers, left untouched by Peuker as the number of people in the church dwindled. There were numerous families recorded there whose children had been baptised in the church but had long ago stopped coming to services. We wrote thousands of letters, inviting them to come back to the church, and many responded. The congregation grew steadily. After two years we had a membership roll of 5,000, double what it had been at Peuker's death.

The names on the roll were of people who had made a formal commitment to the church and supported it financially by regularly giving a contribution to church funds. In the same two years, the income of the church rose from 250,000 lei per annum to 600,000 lei.

As our income rose we were able to begin much needed restoration of the church. Soon the building echoed to the sound of builders and carpenters as years of neglect were gradually dealt with. Eventually, to provide extra seating accommodation for our growing congregation, we built a new balcony. The church was built in the closing years of the nineteenth century when there were reckoned to be only 700 believers in Temesvar. Now we were visited each Sunday by worshippers from all over Transylvania.

Eventually, we had to hold our Sunday service at nine o'clock and again at eleven o'clock. Both were packed, and we had to install loudspeakers to relay the proceedings to people who could not get closer than the corridors and stairways of the building.

One of the most encouraging developments was the number of children and young people coming to the church. The number of confirmations increased steadily. In Peuker's time the church was attended only by old people. There was no sudden rush. From none at all we had ten children in the congregation, then ten more, and so gradually, in twos and threes, the young people came. When we reached fifty, we rejoiced; later, we had a hundred and later even more.

The growth of the church did not happen all at once. But as our numbers grew, the renewal in the life of the congregation for which we had prayed and worked began to be a reality. We began to be a family, to belong to each other in a profound way. Some joined the church out of a need for solidarity, as a means of defending their identity against a society that placed them at a disadvantage. Many who joined for such reasons found in the family of God a much deeper sense of belonging.

A powerful incentive in our rebirth was the fact

that the centenary of the church was approaching. A hundred years before, the church had been re-established after its destruction by the Turks. 'We must rebuild our church to begin the new century,' I urged, 'just as we began to build one hundred years ago.' The idea captured the imagination of the congregation; the impending centenary was a constant topic of conversation and excitement.

The renewal of the congregation was not to the credit of the new pastor. It came about because as a congregation, as a family of the people of God, the church was seeking to be obedient to him, to discover what he wanted us to be doing. Long before it leaped into the forefront of world news as an initiator in toppling the Ceausescu regime, our congregation in Temesvar was a revolutionary organisation. That is what the Church is always called upon to be in whatever time and place. It is a revolution that starts in the souls of people.

6

THE GATHERING STORM

'Pastor Tokes, you are giving me cause for concern.'

Bishop Papp sat perched upright in his chair, looking at me severely over the broad polished wooden desk. The desk seemed almost too large for so small a man, as if the furniture had been made to a slightly different scale. My face remained neutral. It would be a brave man who smiled at the bishop's short stature. He was extraordinarily sensitive on the subject. He avoided preaching from the pulpit, for example. He claimed it was because he suffered from vertigo. But everybody knew that it was because, measured against the massive proportions of our pulpits, he would have looked somewhat ridiculous.

'Cause for *considerable* concern,' the bishop expanded.

I coughed deferentially. 'In what regard?'

'You are permitting the membership to grow too quickly. You are drawing too much attention to the church.'

'It is hard to prevent them coming, Bishop.'

'You could stop them. It is you they come to hear. The city is full of talk about the new preacher at the Reformed Church. Your fine speaking voice.'

'What is happening is happening by the hand of God, Bishop. Perhaps he makes use of skills he gave me. But it is not because of me that the people come.'

'That is not for you to say!' Papp snapped, then adopted a more conciliatory tone. 'It is a temptation, Laszlo. Every pastor experiences it when he begins. People look to you as an authority, as a man of God. There's power there. Don't allow yourself to be led astray from your vocation.'

There was something distasteful about these summonses to the bishop's palace in Nagyvarad. Each time, as I arrived at the drab building with its two ornate towers, built by the Hungarians who had built Nagyvarad, I knew what I was in for. The pretext was always one of concern, usually regarding the wellbeing of the Church, and always wrapped up in some kind of spiritual exhortation. Often he delivered a lecture on Christian leadership. Sometimes the threats were less veiled than at other times, but it was always obvious that the meeting was a heavy-handed attempt to discipline me.

Relating to Laszlo Papp was always a delicate matter, because he was so sensitive. Like many very small men, he coveted power and was rigorous in suppressing those he had overtaken on his way to the bishop's palace – his surveillance of Peuker was only one example.

It was essential to communicate respect to him. Nothing enraged Papp more than the suspicion that people were laughing at him. A colleague of mine once smiled during a lecture being given by Papp at the Theological Institute in Kolozsvar. The bishop immediately instituted disciplinary proceedings against him, and only abandoned them when my colleagues assured him that he had been laughing, not at him, but at somebody who had fallen asleep in the front row.

He was inordinately fond of ceremonials and ritual, and his entry into a room was usually a major theatrical event. To be given Papp's hand to kiss was a great honour. However, a word from him was a dubious favour. If he was gracious to you and spoke pleasantries, your reputation in the Church hierarchy immediately improved: 'He has the ear of the bishop,' people said, and treated you accordingly. But if he said something inconsequential or slightly hostile, it was a signal that he was planning some kind of discipline or criticism against you. Papp knew very well the impact his words made and took a malevolent delight in watching people's reactions.

His most effective weapon was his frequent references to his contacts with the Ceausescu dynasty and the support he received from the regime, the Securitate and the official State newspaper in Bucharest.

My interview was clearly at an end. Papp nodded and extended his hand. I got to my feet, suddenly aware of my six-foot height, and said goodbye.

'Remember what I have said, Pastor Tokes,' he admonished. 'I do not speak only for myself. I have contacts with the Ceausescu family, you know.'

I tried not to stoop as I left.

It was not surprising that the developments in the church at Temesvar should have brought me to the attention of the authorities. After the Revolution we were astonished to find out the extent of the

surveillance since our arrival in the town that the
Securitate carried out on us. It is possible that they
even used sophisticated electronic devices.

They kept out of sight, however. In Dej, I had
been threatened, harassed and constantly pres-
sured by the Securitate. Now my chief Securitate
spy was Laszlo Papp. From my arrival at the church
in 1986 to my departure, I never saw a Securitate
man in my office. They were present at Sunday
services, visited the presbyters and questioned
people with whom I was in close contact. But they
did not approach me. At Dej I had made public
outside Romania the persecution I was receiving;
this time, the Securitate and the authorities were
changing their tactics.

Of course the authorities were likely to take an
interest in anything that strengthened the spirit of
the people and drew them together. Ceausescu's
regime was a regime of separation, forbidding spontaneous gatherings, dividing communities, even
separating husband and wife under the rigorous
laws dictating where trained people could work.

For this reason it was not surprising that one
aspect of our church life which attracted particular
attention was our ecumenical work.

One of the striking characteristics of Temesvar,
and Banat region in which it lies, is the good relationships that exist between the various ethnic
groups. The chequered history of Transylvania has
left significant ethnic communities of Hungarians,
Romanians, Germans and also some Serbs, Slovaks,
Czechs, Bulgarians, Moslems, Jews and Gypsies.
Many of these groups know the languages of some
of the others, and between the different ethnic

groups there is tolerance and understanding. It is a tradition. The same is true of the Christian denominations represented in the area. There is a cosmopolitanism about Banat that you do not find in more easterly parts of Romania.

There has always been a good relationship between the various churches, both between individual church members and at official level. Three times a year the metropolitan of the Orthodox Church invited the other church leaders in the city to a reception; the Orthodox Church was the largest church in Temesvar and the metropolitan was like a patriarch among the old churches.

It is appropriate that there should be these good relationships as the Hungarian population in Temesvar is such a mixed community. The city is a centre of Roman Catholicism, a legacy of the Habsburg rule. Today half the Hungarian Reformed Community make mixed marriages, mainly with Catholics, some with Orthodox. Sometimes when their children came to church we had to teach them Hungarian, which is the official language of our Church.

This does not imply a hostility to Romanians and their language. The reason our pastors use Hungarian exclusively in the major services of the Church first because it is our mother tongue, and also because under Ceausescu, every attempt was made to force us to use Romanian as the language of worship. To have done so would have been to accept the same State domination of our Church that we were protesting against in other ways. To have appeased the State on that point would have been like inviting the camel to put one foot in the tent – soon the invasion would have been absolute.

On a day-to-day, personal level, we were sorry to have to take this stand. Wherever possible we used Romanian; for example when a Hungarian and a Romanian married, we would hold parts of the service in Romanian, and also when a Romanian was being buried. When Romanians were being confirmed we explained everything in Romanian as well as Hungarian. And of course in individual teaching, counselling, praying or simply chatting with Romanians, I spoke their language.

In the context of a mixed and tolerant community, I proposed to make the ecumenical life of Temesvar an everyday reality, not just an affair of formal receptions between high-ranking clergy.

'I want to invite each church in turn to visit us,' I told the presbytery. 'Not just its priests or clergy, but the whole congregation as well. We will have a communion festival together. I will preach and so will the visiting priest. There will be hymn singing from both traditions, and we will invite the believers to take part with songs and poems.'

It was agreed that we would begin by inviting the Roman Catholic Church. We felt that as the Reformed Church came into being out of the Catholic Church, it was entirely appropriate that we should extend our hands to those from whom we had been separated by history. We decided to hold this, our first ecumenical festival, on October 31st – the day that Luther launched the Reformation, and a great holiday in Transylvania.

The regime did not allow bishops to be appointed in the Catholic churches, so it was the deputy bishop, Sebastian Kreuter, who accepted the invitation. He was a German, and his church was made up of German and Hungarian Catholics. The event would be not only an opportunity to make contact with the Roman Catholics but also with the German population.

But before October arrived, other events had dominated our lives.

In March 1988, Ceausescu had announced the plan that was to arouse the horror and indignation of people in countries all round the world. Bucharest was already grievously damaged, its heart wrenched out to make room for the dictator's arrogant monument to himself. Forty thousand residents of the old city had been forcibly rehoused to achieve it. That was only a beginning.

The plan for village 'systematisation' meant the demolition of 8,000 villages over the next twelve years. By the end of the century, the inhabitants of half of Romania's villages would be moved to the cities where they would live in apartment blocks and commute to the farms to work each day. And other cities, too, would be rebuilt like Bucharest. Churches, ancient monuments and long-established dwellings would be replaced by the bleak prison-like apartment blocks.

The cultural consequences were almost unimaginable. Communities that had grown over centuries would disappear in days. A priceless heritage or architecture, art, community and an entire way of life would disappear.

The consequences for society were incalculable. It would mean the effective extermination of much of the Hungarian community in Transylvania. The German community, already diminished, would dwindle even further. The quality of life would be immeasurably lowered – we knew the shoddiness of Ceausescu's socialist apartment blocks, the gaps in the walls, the damp that could never be dealt with because of fundamental flaws in design. And of course, concentrating the community in large units made the task of the Securitate much easier.

'Systematisation', heralded as the dawn of a new Utopian agricultural efficiency, was really a way of systematising people. The peasants were the last homogeneous social category in Romania, and it was Ceausescu's ambition to break them. He intended to remodel Romanian society into the new socialist society – dependent and manipulated.

The implementation of the policy raised a storm of protest in the West. The first villages to be demolished were in the Bucharest area. It is probable that the uproar from the West caused Ceausescu to rethink his policy; apart from some villages near Tirgu-Mures, the systematisation programme went no further. But there was continuing destruction in the cities. Indeed, it could be argued that the village plan had been prepared for by less publicised attacks on the cities. In the early 1970s, for example, the old Hungarian quarter in Kolozsvar was bulldozed and the people rehoused elsewhere.

Janos Molnar, who had been a leader among the student dissidents at Kolozsvar and a close friend of mine, was now in the Arad deanery of which the Temesvar church was a member. He was living in the town of Sebis and had been trying to emigrate for three years. After being suspended for a year at the Theological Institute, he was later expelled from the Church, a year before my own expulsion; but whereas Nagy expelled me illegally and by intimidation, Papp expelled Janos by pretending he was ill and needed to rest. He relieved him of his duties for twelve months, and then sent him to 'convalesce' in Sebis. There are only about 150 believers there and it is an intensely anti-Hungarian town. Its Hungarian population was decimated in the massacre of 1848 and few Hungarians live there now.

The Molnar family had three terrible years in Sebis. Their son was persecuted at school so severely that he became mentally disturbed. Janos applied to Bucharest, to the Foreign Ministry and the Hungarian Embassy, but his requests for emigration were denied.

Janos and I decided to organise a protest against the village plan, to attempt to pressurise the Church authorities to speak against it. We were under no illusions as to where the loyalties of the bishops lay. We considered there was a clear strategy apparent in the Church. The increasing restriction in the number of theological students at Kolozsvar was in preparation for a future church organised into a few giant parishes needing far fewer pastors. On the State's part, the plan was to destroy physically the parishes by bulldozing the buildings. The two went hand-in-hand.

We resolved to protest as vehemently as we could and mobilise as much protest as possible. We both knew that this would bring the wrath of the Securitate down upon us, and that our bishops would help them in their persecution. But we were so angered by the threat to Romanian village life that we did not count the risks. It was an injustice of such proportions that we believed if we did not protest the stones would cry out against us. The greatest enemy was fear – Ceausescu's strongest weapon. But even the Securitate were only human beings.

Our plan was to appeal to the leaders of every denomination to enter into dialogue with the State to stop the destruction of the villages. We felt that the morality of faith entitled us to make such an appeal.

Next we turned to the leaders of our own church. Through the summer of 1988, we talked with people in all the thirteen deaneries of the two Reformed dioceses. Between us, we had friends all over Transylvania. I talked with the eight deaneries in the Transylvania diocese, and Janos with the five in the diocese of Nagyvarad. There was a good response. We were given undertakings wherever we went that our friends would raise the matter in September at the monthly deanery meeting. It was a carefully coordinated campaign, and we secured many promises that the village destruction proposals would be discussed at the same time in every deanery.

On September 6th Janos and I introduced the subject at our own deanery meeting at Arad. Janos had prepared a statement which I supported. He read it to the meeting.

> . . . Our church communities cannot be indifferent to these programmes. We, the deaneries of the Reformed Church, propose to resist these programmes and make contact with other denominations and fight alongside them. There may be economic and political reasons for them, but we believe the moral consequences are so incalculable that the churches must fight to gain a compromise.

Among the demands of our proposal, we asked that no church be demolished without being replaced by another, that people be rehoused near their old homes, that new housing be comparable in quality with the old, that the distribution of the denominations be preserved. And we asked that the Churches appoint delegates to work with the authorities to ensure that these demands were carried out. We called on the Churches 'to unite and salvage what is possible in the interests of ordinary village people, to try to save historical buildings and churches, and generally lessen the damage that systematisation is causing to the country'.

We asked that the document be signed by the deanery and that it then be sent to Bishop Papp.

Our hope had been that at least several pastors would sign it. To our surprise, the meeting voted to send it to the bishop – not in the name of individual pastors, but in the name of the deanery. Though the majority in favour was not great, there was much enthusiasm. Some proposed that a copy of the document be sent to every church district in Romania. I proposed that we should pray every Sunday in our churches for the threatened villages.

'After all,' I said, 'if we pray for South Africa and the Third World we can pray for our own villages too . . .'

The courage of those who signed the manifesto should not be underestimated. The deanery of Arad had a poor reputation. It was small, representing only thirty parishes. It was the place you came to if you did not have the ability or the connections to be a pastor in one of the important cities or villages. Many pastors were in Arad deanery as a punishment; I myself was there as a disciplinary measure, and some of the pastors I knew were there for drunkenness and other misdemeanours. Those who supported our statement were doubly brave, not only because they risked the wrath of the regime, but because they risked rejection by their fellow pastors.

The document was sent to Bishop Laszlo Papp. We did not have to wait long for his response. Within twenty-four hours, every member of the deanery had been visited by the Securitate and cross-examined about the events of the meeting. On September 12th, Janos Molnar, myself and a third member of the deanery who had led the voting in favour of our document were summoned to the bishop's office in Nagyvarad.

The bishop's personal office is at the end of a suite of rooms, each leading into the next, as is common in Hungarian buildings; in effect there is a series of anterooms. The three of us were told to wait in different rooms so that we could not talk to each other. One by one we were called into Papp's office where we were interrogated for an hour each by the bishop, his assistant Eszenyi and the inspector from the Department of Cults. As each of us came out, we were led to our rooms to make sure we did not pass information to the others.

This unwieldy system broke down quite easily. While Janos was being interrogated I asked my guard if I could go to the lavatory. He refused, saying I might be planning to meet somebody. I sat in some discomfort for a while, then the guard disappeared. A few moments later, I took the opportunity to go downstairs and across the court-yard to the lavatory. Emerging a few moments later,

I met Janos who had been allowed by *his* guard to go to the lavatory. We exchanged a few hurried words.

'It's difficult,' said Janos. 'They won't believe that you didn't write the document. They think I just supported you. I've told them it was the other way.'

'What sort of questions did they ask you?'

'I think they have you categorised as a rebel,' grinned Janos. At that moment there was a shout from the main building. The guards had discovered we were absent. The deputy bishop came running down the stairs to the lavatory so fast he almost tripped and fell. When he reached us he was crimson-faced. It made the whole affair seem ludicrous at the time, but also tragic. It was the job of our bishop to deal with us privately and defend us against the atheistic state, not to join its representatives sitting in judgment upon us.

Laszlo Papp began my interview with a reference to my application for post-graduate study. 'It would still be possible for you to study abroad,' he said casually. I wondered if it was a threat or a bribe. Certainly his manner was affable.

Suddenly his tone became cold and severe. 'Reports have been made to me,' he said, 'by some members of the community in Temesvar. It is said that your church reconstruction project is running into difficulties.'

'I have heard nothing of it,' I said. 'It is not true.'

'And they say that there are financial irregularities.'

For a moment there was silence in the room. The trams in the street outside roared past. The inspector from the Department of Cults watched me coldly. I looked past them at the walnut bookcase,

its neat rows of theology and church proceedings
gathering dust behind the glass.

'If you provide me with the report in question,'
I said firmly, 'I will investigate. I know of no
irregularities.'

The bishop consulted his papers. 'Your father.
His work has been published abroad. Do you know
the details?'

'No,' I said.

Bishop Papp sat back in his chair and looked at
me. 'Now – the document that I have received from
your deanery meeting. Tell me more about it.'

I gave an account of the meeting and how the
document had originated.

'But that is not how it happened, is it, Mr Tokes?
In fact, you wrote the document.'

I sighed. 'No. I have explained. Mr Molnar wrote
it, I made a few corrections. I support the document
entirely. It is a most moderate argument.'

The inspector leaned forward. 'Mr Tokes, your
career in Dej was characterised by opposition to the
authorities and to those who were your seniors in
the Church. You were twice disciplined and you
were thrown out of the Church. Now you are doing
the same things in Temesvar.'

They had made their minds up. It was not enough
that I should acknowledge my full support for
Janos's document. They would not be convinced
that I had not written it myself.

That was frustrating, but much more frustrating
was the patronising sermon that the bishop
preached to us all before we were allowed to leave.

'The State is for us in the place of God,' he told us.
'For the Church in our times, the State's decrees are
like the Scriptures. It is not for us to reject them or to

criticise the decisions of President Ceausescu.' We had no choice but to listen to his panegyric as he droned on, dwarfed by the Inspector of Cults sitting bored at his side.

'If the State should even decide that the great church in Nagyvarad should be demolished – if for the good of the people that were necessary – it would not matter. The first Christians worshipped under the sky and in the catacombs. Our faith does not depend on stones and mortar. We can be good Christians without churches.'

I felt the same bitter taste in my mouth that I always felt after an admonition from the bishop. Then he switched back into character. 'If you do not conduct yourselves properly,' he warned, 'anything might happen. Don't you care about your families? Don't you want to live in peace?'

A picture of Edit and Mate came into my mind. The bishop was still lecturing us. 'We understand that you are young and did not realise what effect your activities could have. A pastor's duty is to preach and to leave the politics to others.'

We went back to our homes, and later we each received a brief note, officially warning us about our attitudes at the meeting. The warning meant nothing. But we knew it was only the beginning. Later still we heard that none of our friends who had promised to raise the matter at their deaneries had done so. They had all been too frightened of the possible results. We had been the only people to raise the matter at a deanery meeting.

On October 6th, I was called to the office of Mr Teperdel, the Inspector of Cults, and told that an anonymous complaint had been made against me.

It charged me with incitement against the State
(because of the Arad document), nationalism (because of our decision to use the Hungarian language
in our services), mismanagement of the building
finances and various minor complaints. Teperdel
harangued me, threatened me and humiliated me,
while declaring, 'We have always had great respect
for the Church and have always guaranteed its
freedom.'

Afterwards I wrote to Bishop Papp describing
what had happened, and asking him respectfully to
protect me from 'external and internal misunder-
standings and false accusations in the future'. But it
was clear that since the document of September 6th,
Papp and I were locked in battle.

On October 31st, we had the joint festival we had
planned with the Catholic church. It was a wonderful, festive occasion. About twenty Catholic and
Reformed students recited poems by a Transylvanian poet. A German Catholic writer who is also an
opera singer sang a song while a Hungarian Catholic woman played the organ. A Catholic priest was
present who was half German, half Hungarian: his
parents were half Reformed and half Catholic.

In every way it was an ecumenical occasion. We
invited all the intellectuals of the city. It was a great
success, the first time anything like it had happened
in Temesvar.

The results were immediate and unpleasant.
From that time on the serious persecution of our
church and our parish began. The Securitate found
it hard to understand what the purpose of our
meeting was. We were minority churches organising a joint activity. We had not invited the Orthodox
Church, the State Church, to be present. But the

inter-church receptions held in the city were hosted by the Orthodox Church. So what were our reasons for meeting on our own? It was highly suspicious; what did we want, what were our demands as minority Churches?

The Catholic deputy bishop Kreuter received a visit from the Securitate, and was criticised severely for accepting the invitation. One night the Catholic pastor who had preached came to see me.

'Be careful,' he warned. 'The Securitate are watching you closely now. I've already been harassed. In fact I cannot visit you again. It would be too dangerous for both of us. I'm under surveillance.'

The ones who suffered most were the students who had taken part. They were threatened with expulsion from the university and criticised at a public assembly for collaborating with the church. Four of them were expelled from the Hungarian theatre group. This was the last surviving Hungarian cultural group in the university, already struggling against many restrictions and pressures; with the loss of its four most talented actors, it was unable to continue. On top of all that, each student who participated in our meeting was cross-examined by the Securitate and given a harsh warning.

I felt personally responsible for what had happened to them. I wrote to Bishop Papp again, condemning the methods of the university leaders and the Securitate. I called on the bishop to defend these young people and give them protection. The response was another summons to Nagyvarad where I was subjected to a furious attack by a member of the bishop's staff, Mr Eszenyi.

'This is a final warning,' he said angrily. 'If you continue your activities with the young people and hold further services of this nature with other churches in Temesvar, you will be removed from the city altogether.' After the meeting, I received a letter from Bishop Papp in which he repeated Eszenyi's threats. He also banned, not only in Temesvar, but in the entire diocese, any youth activity, even the formation of youth choirs. Only members of the presbytery were to be allowed to sing solos in church or recite poetry.

It was an appalling letter for any bishop to write. Papp was bringing in a prohibition that no state worker was bound by. This was a draconian measure aimed at crippling the ecumenical programme and ensuring that organised Christian work among young people would be severely handicapped. It was a naked threat from the regime, though it bore the signature of the Bishop of Nagyvarad.

I ignored the threat, but not for the first time grieved that my bishop was not prepared to protect ecumenical initiative or youth activities that are guaranteed by the Constitution.

In November, the authorities moved to stop the church rebuilding programme. This would have been a major problem for us. The rebuilding was much more than a practical solution to an increasing space problem. It was something that bound the church together, that built up our identity as a community of people. To stop the rebuilding would have been a serious setback to our growth as a fellowship. It was also illegal: only the disciplinary council of the Church could have made such a ruling legally. I refused to obey.

The winter of 1988–9 was as bitter as the previous year's. Our work in the church was hampered by numerous harassments by the Securitate.

Then Janos Molnar in Sebis received an unexpected letter from Bucharest informing him that his application to emigrate had been approved. After years of refusal, the bureaucracy had suddenly leaped into action. Janos and his family were issued with passports and allowed to leave Romania. They made their home in Hungary. The regime had disposed of one of the three Arad dissidents.

I tried to discuss the situation with the third member of our trio questioned in the bishop's office. To my sorrow, he had changed his attitude completely. Having enthusiastically voted for the manifesto in September, he was now interested only in conforming to the regime's wishes. He wanted nothing to do with our plans to oppose the village demolitions.

That left only Laszlo Tokes to be dealt with.

We had decided that the next ecumenical festival should be with the Orthodox Church. Early in the spring of 1989 I went to visit the Orthodox metropolitan, and also the priest of the Orthodox Church a few hundred yards from my own. I asked for the metropolitan's approval of a similar meeting with the Orthodox believers. They both agreed willingly. It was a great encouragement to be given their support after the Securitate had persecuted the students and Catholics who had taken part in the previous festival.

There was still no major development from the bishop in response to the events of September.

There were certainly many harassments. I was summoned again to Nagyvarad where Eszenyi accused me of incompetence, disloyalty and faithlessness.

'You are a bad pastor, you are destroying your own church,' he ranted. I reminded myself that he was lying and tried not to allow it to hinder my work.

On March 3rd, I received a message from a relative in Nagyvarad. It said preparations were being made in the bishop's office to have me dismissed from my post in Temesvar. The grounds for my dismissal were the statement I was said to have prepared for the Arad deanery meeting in September.

I decided to make sure that whatever happened I would have an opportunity to speak out.

In Canada, my brother Istvan was approached by Michel Clair, a former minister in the Quebec government. He was deeply concerned about the situation of the Hungarian minority in Romania, and Istvan was a well-known lobbyist for the cause. Clair wanted to set up a fact-finding trip to Romania, and asked Istvan who he should contact. He replied that I and our father would be very important sources.

Clair teamed up with a photographer, Rejean Roy, and a complicated plan was devised for the team to enter Romania in early March, film interviews with me and others, and smuggle the tapes out. They arrived at the church in secrecy, bearing a signed photograph of Istvan's daughter sent as a sign of good faith. We filmed an interview in the church.

Afterwards, Clair and Roy went on to Kolozsvar,

but things went wrong. Their activities aroused the interest of the Securitate, and they were arrested and given five hours to leave Romania. The tapes, however, had already been smuggled out by friends. Meanwhile, in Temesvar the pressure continued.

When the call came from Nagyvarad on March 11th, I was prepared. In a way, I was tranquil, almost as if I were watching a game. I knew that the bishop's staff had no idea I knew what was going to happen. The decision was announced with a flourish, but I listened calmly. I knew that events were now moving to a climax, that the conflict could only become worse. But I knew that God was with me and I felt a great peace.

The bishop became angrier as I became calmer. To a long list of accusations, I simply replied, 'That's not true, but I won't argue with you.' When told the news of my dismissal, I said, 'All right, thank you.'

I was stalling to gain time. Had I protested or refused to go there and then, the procedures would have speeded up. I wanted to go back to Temesvar to begin to prepare my defence.

When I was appointed to Temesvar after my struggles and experiences at Dej, I vowed that if I could be a pastor once again, I would not conform in any way to the bishop and the regime. I knew that the whole sequence of meetings and threats and reprimands was just a charade. They were trying to shut me up. And I decided that in Temesvar I was not going to give up. This time I was going to take the fight right to the end.

At home, I convened the presbytery. They were outraged. They drafted a declaration that they did not wish me to leave and we sent it to the bishop. But the bishop did not believe that I would have the temerity to refuse his decision and resist his authority.

On March 31st, I was called to Nagyvarad again and presented with a formal notice of suspension. 'You will receive a visit from Dean Kovacs. You will make arrangements for the presbytery to meet him.' I was to vacate the manse at Temesvar and move to Mineu, a tiny village in the mountains to the north of Kolozsvar, far away from Temesvar.

It was a very clever move showing the same cunning that had got rid of Janos Molnar. Open expulsion would have provoked a Church incident and considerable interest from the West. Refusal to accept a bishop's instruction, however, would look like deliberate disobedience on my part. The skilled foresight that had ensured I was kept a probationary pastor had kept me firmly under the direct jurisdiction of the bishop. At that time, seventy per cent of the pastors in his diocese – about two hundred – had never been promoted from probationary status and were still directly answerable to Papp.

I tried to get more information, but was told nothing more. This was the bishop's method; to rule by fear and intimidation. He governed the church by telephone. The office telephone bill every month was between ten and twenty thousand lei – between three and six hundred pounds. Very little was written down, except what would incriminate others. So there was no public record of his threats and illegal actions.

Two days later, I had virtually forgotten the warning about Kovacs. I returned to Temesvar with the news about Mineu, and Edit and I talked about our next step. Neither of us had any intention of doing other than resisting the bishop's demands. If we had no other reason, the prospects for our congregation if I was removed were bleak. Papp would ensure that the next pastor was compliant and willing to take the church back to the old ways. In the twenty-four hours after my return, I did not have time to brief the presbytery about the meeting.

On Sunday morning I was in the church office, ready to preach as usual. My father was with me. He had come to conduct a christening during the service. Kovacs entered the office with a small delegation and announced he would be preaching that morning.

It was like an invasion. The presbytery were horrified. I tried to reason with Kovacs. 'Mr Kovacs, you are a dean and you have the legal right to preach in my pulpit. But I beg you not to do so. If you preach, you will be helping the bishop to do something which is wrong. You know why I am suspended. You know the history of this situation. It is unworthy of you to do this.'

He was immovable. I knew the man well. He was appointed to a village church by Papp as a personal favour, and his appointment as dean was also only by the bishop's pleasure. He held his office only while Laszlo Papp was pleased with him. His son, too, was hoping to study at the Theological Institute, and the bishop had made it clear to Kovacs that his son's career depended on the father's conforming. In this way Papp controlled people.

'If it means so much to you, do it,' I said resignedly.

While we were talking, the members of the presbytery were telling the believers in church what was happening and the news spread quickly through the congregation. When Kovacs appeared there was an uproar of protest. Our congregation was a large one and the noise so great that Kovacs was unable to make himself heard.

I entered the pulpit and managed to quieten them enough for me to speak. While I was appealing for calm, I recognised in the congregation Archbishop Borsi, a dignitary close to Laszlo Papp. I had not seen him in the office earlier. *He's here to keep an eye on Kovacs*, I realised with some amusement, and decided to thwart at least part of the intrigue.

'We welcome here this morning Dean Kovacs from Arad. And we also have with us in the congregation Archbishop Borsi from Nagyvarad.' I could not see Kovacs's reaction, but hoped I had spoiled his composure a little. 'Revd Kovacs will be preaching this morning.'

There was a wave of antagonism. I raised my hand. 'Please, let Revd Kovacs speak. He has come to preach the word of God. It is still God's word, whoever expounds it. Be attentive and listen quietly, and afterwards both I and the dean will explain what is going on.'

And so the dean succeeded in preaching his sermon and demonstrating the power of the bishop to control my pulpit.

During the service my father conducted the baptism, but the atmosphere was edgy and disturbed. When I stood up to speak again, I looked down at a sea of angry faces.

I summarised the situation briefly and calmly. The bishop had suspended me, I told them, and I was to be transferred to Mineu. The presbytery had decided to support me in my opposition to this. The bishop was acting illegally and autocratically. 'I ask that you too will support us in our stand,' I concluded.

I gestured to Kovacs to speak in his turn. He rose to his feet and addressed the crowded church. 'Leave the church. Go home. I am here to speak with the presbytery. The pastor's business does not concern you.'

It was an unbelievable error of judgment. The congregation reacted predictably. They refused to leave. There was a danger that Kovacs might be physically attacked – Borsi had already made good his escape. My father went into the pulpit and tried to pacify them, quoting Scripture and appealing to them to be calm.

Soon the two dignitaries and their delegation had no choice but to leave. The congregation followed them to their cars and cheered and chanted as they drove off. Later, a petition opposing my removal was sent to Nagyvarad bearing the signatures of the congregation.

It was the beginning of a heady realisation; that it was possible to defeat injustice, that the powerful and corrupt could be driven off. On that day, our congregation in Temesvar began the long fight against the will of the dictator, the will of the bishop.

7

FIGHTING AGAINST DICTATORS

Now began a story of eight long months of resistance, in which time Bishop Papp, the Securitate, the Department of Cults in Bucharest, the Inspectorate of Religions in Temesvar, the militia and the town leaders all tried everything in their power to remove me or persuade the presbytery to evict me themselves.

On April 5th, I wrote to Bishop Papp, stating that what had happened the previous Sunday was an illegal attempt by the diocese to occupy my church. I emphasised that there were no circumstances in which I was prepared to hand over my church.

In the next few days I wrote to every church leader in Temesvar. It was a gesture of fellowship. I knew we were not alone. We had good links with the other churches and were familiar with the sufferings our brothers and sisters in other denominations were experiencing. Mine was not the only voice raised against the regime's treatment of the churches. Nor was the Hungarian Reformed Church the only church whose leadership was serving (or fearing) the atheistic state. For example, while the ancient Orthodox Churches of Bucharest and elsewhere fell under Ceausescu's bulldozers, not a single Orthodox bishop raised a voice in protest.

So I wrote to the church leaders, telling them about our situation and asking for their prayers. I wrote to them as fellow combatants in the struggle of the Christian Church in Romania. On April 8th, I wrote to Bishop Papp again. Drawing the comparison with what had happened in Dej and listing the names of those who had been involved in both cases, I went on:

> I will resist by any means. I only ask one thing: leave me in peace to carry on my work, and do not curtail our freedom that is ensured by the Constitution, the statutes and my contract.

My letter concluded with a statement that Edit and myself had discussed at length and had already revealed in my letters to the church leaders:

> I henceforth begin a voluntary self-exile, and I will only leave my flat, which provides a certain amount of security, to carry out my duties as a pastor.

The bishop's response was to launch a disciplinary investigation against me and attempt to secure a civil eviction order. I consulted lawyers – one was my uncle and another was from Tirgu-Mures. They agreed with me that the suspension and transfer were illegal. On April 13th, there was a disciplinary hearing. I was not present to defend myself. Several days later I received a letter announcing that the conclusion of the hearing was a reaffirmation of my suspension.

The civil legal arguments went backwards and forwards. In the meantime, I carried on my work. The church reconstruction programme progressed. We had one major disappointment. Shortly after the attempted occupation of our church, I tried to continue the discussions about the next ecumenical festival, in which the Orthodox Church had agreed to be involved. There had been a complete change of attitude. When I went to see the metropolitan, I was told he was unavoidably engaged. I tried to telephone, but was constantly told that nobody in the office was able to speak to me. The embarrassment was almost palpable. Eventually I abandoned my attempts and reported to the presbytery that the festival could not take place.

I had no doubt that the Securitate had put pressure on the church, and that the leaders were alarmed at the prospect of being publicly, and unpopularly, associated with a church that was now openly in conflict with the Communist regime. It was a great sadness to us.

The ecumenical festivals were the reason for another dramatic development in April. Kossuth Radio in Hungary transmitted a special Sunday service in which they read the contents of my letter to the bishop complaining about the treatment of the students and his response. Although it was illegal to listen to foreign radio broadcasts, Kossuth Radio could be easily picked up in Transylvania and had a wide audience. Now my conflict with the Bishop of Nagyvarad was known of throughout Transylvania.

In fact the ban on ecumenical activities was thwarted in an unexpected way. From that time, Sunday by Sunday, the congregation at our morning service was swollen by many new faces. Among the people who came were many Catholics and members of other churches. It became an ecumenical meeting, and much interest was generated in what was happening at our church. It was a passive, peaceful demonstration by the people. And the Securitate did not know how to handle it.

The other proscribed activity – cultural and youth work in the church – was also thwarted. We held special services in the church in which we invited students to take part. They were not actors, and their contribution formed only part of the programme, so the services were neither cultural events nor services specifically for the young. Papp's demand that young people be forbidden to recite poetry in church we simply disobeyed. It was a flagrantly illegal request and contravened basic social rights established by law.

Through the summer, Hungarian Radio broadcast at least one item about me and the church every week. The Westerners who had befriended us while I was at Dej also reported what was happening. Radio Free Europe, Voice of America and the BBC World Service all carried items about me, which not only informed the West about what was happening, but also gave Romanians information denied them by the government.

On the other hand, anonymous threats, which first began appearing in the spring, now became more frequent. Mysterious telephone messages and other warnings all bore the same message: if I did not stop my attack on the bishop, I would be in great personal danger.

My correspondence with Nagyvarad continued. I emphasised that the bishop's actions not only contradicted the laws of the Church, but broke the Romanian Labour Code. I rejected any decision to move me to Mineu. On May 19th, I lodged an official appeal against my transfer. I pointed out that whereas the bishop was proceeding against me on the basis that I was behaving illegally, I had always conducted my activities within the law. I quoted the statutes of the Reformed Church, and the statutes and Labour Code of Romania. I attached copies of relevant legal statutes and cases urging the bishop either to withdraw his order or place the whole matter in the hands of a properly constituted church council, before which the case could be fully argued by both sides. Papp refused.

On May 21st, I preached on the text: 'We must obey God rather than men' (Acts 5:29). I described the scene; Peter and the apostles before the Sanhedrin, those high priests who wanted to silence the free spirit.

I drew the obvious comparison between their situation and our own. We were in a conflict situation, and conflicts always brought discord and crisis. That was what had caused Peter's uncertainty and personal crisis and Judas's betrayal of Jesus.

'We all have to stand in front of the Sanhedrin once,' I said. There was an attentive silence as I continued. 'God has to be given precedence over man. That is the resolution of the conflict. And thereby we are given the strength of the Holy Spirit.'

I quoted examples: Moses, Daniel, Luther. 'But it is not simply a matter of great issues in history. It has to do with everyday life, how we live each moment of our lives. How often we face questions of whom to side with, whom to support, when to say yes, when to say no. Every day we face the dilemma of how to choose the narrow path instead of the broad one.'

I closed with a verse from 1 Corinthians: 'Be on your guard; stand firm in the faith; be men of courage; be strong. Do everything in love' (1 Cor. 16:13).

The congregation were resolved to support me, come what may. Shortly after the sermon, the presbytery signed a fresh petition to Bishop Papp, appealing against my transfer and asking that I be allowed to remain in Temesvar. They said that as was their statutory right, they now appointed Laszlo Tokes to be a full pastor. But they wished to place the matter in the bishop's hands so that he could formally ratify their election.

They took the petition to Nagyvarad on May 26th, but the bishop would not see them.

At the end of the month I was embroiled in an argument with the bishop over the use of theatre in our church services. I insisted again that his ban on such activities could not be supported from Church law, that the law itself guaranteed freedom for individual parishes to act as they wished, even in opposition to illegally imposed restrictions from Church leaders.

'I asked you not to interfere,' I said. 'I ask you to withdraw the ban on our church activities.'

The letter was written on the day that the Inspector of Religious Affairs in Bucharest had conducted an interrogation of myself and members of the presbytery. He tried to cause conflict between us, threatening to close the presbytery down completely.

The inspector condemned my links with Kossuth

Radio, now broadcasting regular news items about me and our church.

'You are guilty of airing internal presbyterian matters. You have talked freely of things that should be kept private. The restrictions that have been placed upon your services and your transfer to Mineu – these are purely internal matters.'

I answered him angrily, 'What could be more natural than sharing problems and seeking an exchange of opinions? If we share a faith, that faith has to show itself in the sharing of the problems just as much as the joys.'

The inspector demanded that I translate into Romanian the letters that Kossuth Radio had broadcast.

'And we have this,' he said, producing a letter I recognised. It was one I had written to the World Reformed Church Organisation concerning my harassment by the police in March. It had been confiscated by the authorities.

I wrote an account of the meeting and sent it to Bishop Papp. I was determined that he should be confronted at every opportunity with his responsibility: to defend one of his pastors who was being harassed by the State.

The bishop did nothing.

On June 11th, I sat down at my typewriter and wrote yet another letter to Bishop Papp. This time it was an open letter. I poured out all my sorrow and anger. I wrote about my past grievances – the lack of support and even outright threats that were all I had received from the diocese; the attempts to silence me; the crude attempts at bribery including the offer of the Temesvar post.

I had been suspended from my job, given show-trial interrogations, publicly humiliated and accused. The Church authorities had acted according to a principle: 'Remove Laszlo Tokes by any means possible.'

'The ghost of the united clerical and secular power of past centuries comes back to haunt us,' I warned, and pushed the point even nearer home: 'The spirit of Stalinism is very much alive in the Church today.'

I looked around my study in which I had spent most of my time for the past few months. Since my voluntary house-imprisonment, I had only left the house on pastoral business or to conduct funerals. I thought of the great traditions of the church of which I was a pastor. The building in which I sat had been built by Hungarians who would have died to defend their faith from a godless secular enemy. How far from the truth had our bishops fallen, when a pastor could be disciplined for protesting against the arbitrary demolition of churches and for organising youth activities in his church.

'I appeal to you,' I wrote. 'Abandon your road to Damascus. You are destroying the Church. I appeal to you to resign as bishop, immediately, voluntarily and publicly.'

I read the letter through, signed it and sat for a while contemplating what I had done. Then I sighed, placed it in a drawer in my desk, and locked the drawer.

It was at this time that a group of my friends formed themselves into a secret activist group, working to publicise what was going on in Temesvar. It was they who now made it their responsibility to get news out of Romania and into the hands of the Western media.

If the immediate church circle comprised myself, Edit and Mate, the secret group could be called a second circle. It includes members of my family, friends and members of the congregation. They established direct links with Kossuth Radio and the authorities in Budapest. Many who joined that circle knew the risks were grave. Christians had died in Romania for just such activities. Others had been persecuted.

On July 7th, I wrote to the bishop informing him that I had now completed three months of voluntary self-exile and intended to resume my normal activities.

There was much to do in the church and in the city. Ceausescu's terrible policies had brought Romania to the edge of starvation. People queued for the most basic food; the shops were empty of virtually everything but row upon row of sickly bottled fruit, and prices rose.

Our church had been increasingly involved since the mid-1980s in food distribution, and the harsh winters and food rationing had made such work extremely important. With the help of friends from abroad who supplied food, we were able to help people in need. Because there were heavy restrictions on what could be sent into Romania by post, our friends had to bring it in by road, often at considerable personal risk. Many border guards refused to concede that Ceausescu's perfect socialist state could be in need of anything at all.

The food problems of Romania affected Temesvar slightly less seriously than elsewhere because the city is a food-producing centre with a number of factories. This meant that we were able to give help to villagers who travelled in from some distance knowing that meat was available in Temesvar. Medicine, too, was distributed.

We did not restrict our help to Reformed believers. We saw ourselves as having a responsibility to everybody. Nor were we the only church doing this; other congregations were receiving food and distributing it. As a pastor I saw such work as being very appropriate for a Christian leader. How could one only teach the Bible to starving people, if one could also feed their stomachs? For me, it was a fulfilling of the example I had first received in my mother's kitchen, listening to stories about the grandfathers whom I had never met.

On July 26th, came the event that precipitated the final phase of the conflict.

The Hungarian television programme *Panorama* is a major news and current affairs programme that is received in Transylvania. Reception tends to vary – the best picture can be obtained when the weather is bad – but most of western Romania is able to receive it, though Ceausescu made it illegal to do so. It had a large audience in Romania during July, because newspapers were unobtainable and the only news to be had came by television and radio.

On the evening of July 26th, those watching saw Alajos Chrudinak, the presenter, introduce the film of the interview I had given to the Canadian team in March, just before the bishop's formal announcement of my suspension.

The role of Alajos Chrudinak in the events of 1989 cannot be overestimated. It was he who orchestrated the coverage of our story on Hungarian television and by persistent investigation and reporting kept the issue in the forefront of the news. It is well known that pressure from abroad has often been instrumental in securing the protection and release of dissidents in Eastern Europe; it is certain that Alajos Chrudinak is one of the people responsible for our survival through those final months of persecution.

Another who played a crucial part in publicising our situation in the West was Miklos Kovacs of Budapest, who co-ordinated medical and food aid to Romania, and regularly met me in Temesvar to collect copies of my letters to the church and other documents. These he smuggled out, at great personal risk, and sent to radio stations and organisations such as Keston College in England, who published the information widely. It is true to say that the March interview would not have been possible without the media activity generated by these men and others.

I had told almost nobody about the interview, not even my close friends of the 'second circle'. The Securitate were already treating us quite badly and I had no illusion about their capacity to extract information. It had been a principal of my actions for some time that I said very little about my plans to those who did not need to know.

The interview was filmed in the church in Temesvar and to those watching had obviously been filmed in winter as I was wearing winter clothes. The church was empty. I spoke without passion or rhetoric. When the interview was taking place, I felt a great calm. Though I knew the film would be shown to millions, I spoke as one might speak to a friend or colleague in a private room.

I described the village systematisation scheme and explained its implications. I talked about the effects of Ceausescu's policies already evident in Romanian society – the assault on ethnic minorities, the mass movement of people compulsorily to the cities, the interference and manipulation of the churches by the regime.

Step by step, I said that our homes, our institutions, our human rights were being destroyed. For us Hungarians, it was a deliberate attempt to eradicate our culture. For too long we had been like trees bending in a storm, arguing that it is better to bend than to break. But now that attitude had to end.

'It is our duty to speak out when everybody, including the highest ranks of Church leadership, is silent. There are questions torturing my brother pastors and members of my congregation, and they are too frightened to say anything. I feel an irresistible urge now to say openly all the things I have choked back so many times before. Why should we always build ourselves into this wall of silence? This wall is more solid and impenetrable than the Berlin wall. And I feel somebody should start dismantling this wall.'

Millions had heard me speak on television. I had passed a great borderline. I was now well within that area of dissent in which Ceausescu ruthlessly eliminated his critics. It was entirely possible that I might be the next unexplained casualty.

After the broadcast, we waited to see what the response of the authorities would be. The following day I had one anonymous telephone call. 'You're a man who no longer has a country,' shouted the caller, and slammed the telephone down.

For over three weeks there was silence from the authorities. We joked that everybody was on holiday. It was more likely that they were following a favourite strategy: to put as long a period as possible between an offence and its punishment, so that apprehension mounted and one was never quite sure whether a particular gamble had succeeded or was simply waiting for retribution. The country was governed by fear, and the regime's techniques for inducing fear were unlimited.

My attitude in those months was that I was pushing against a barrier. Bishop Papp and the authorities were persecuting me and my church and I did not know how much longer they would refrain from direct and terrible action. I wanted to push against the barrier and see how far one could go. I wanted to see where were the limits of protest.

The consequences, when they came, were severe. My telephone became curiously unreliable, allowing only incoming calls, so that I could not telephone anybody and the anonymous telephone threats I received regularly could continue. Securitate guards were placed at the entrance to the church building. Our visitors were cross-examined and searched.

On August 15th, I unlocked my desk drawer and took out the letter to Bishop Papp that I had written in June and never posted. In it I had called on him to resign. Now I turned to my typewriter again.

'Two months ago, I wrote an open letter to you. I had second thoughts; I was frightened; I decided it was better not to send it immediately. I hoped the need to send it would never arise. But that hope was without foundation. You, Bishop Papp, are continuing your opportunist and undermining policies towards the Church in general, serving the dictator; and your activities are a danger to our church.'

I typed fluently, my anger spilling on to the paper. 'I do not need to talk about my personal situation, because these other issues are more important. That is why I send you this open letter now. And I call upon you again to change your policies which are destroying our church or resign your title of bishop, to which you have no claim. I know that I speak for the whole Church.'

On August 25th, the bishop's response came. Short, terse and final, the brief note informed me that I was no longer a pastor of the Reformed Church. I would have to vacate the manse, otherwise I would be evicted by force.

The judgment had no legal validity whatsoever. My lawyer, Elod Kincses, immediately appealed on the basis that the Reformed Church's own disciplinary code states that the only way a pastor can be removed is by a court of the Church. Bishop Papp's only justification for his action was that it had the approval of the State's Department of Cults.

The bishop began a scandalous intimidation of the Council, and the lengthy process of securing an ecclesiastically valid eviction order.

My sermon on September 10th was on the subject of 'Perfect love casts out fear.' I spoke of the power of love; how can fear survive if one has love in the biblical sense? Our most frightening times were almost upon us. Two days later, Erno Ujvarossy, the author of the petition opposing my dismissal from Temesvar and one of those who had taken it to Nagyvorad on May 26th, disappeared. He was found dead in a forest six days later with every appearance of foul play.

He was somebody of whom we were all deeply fond. He had been leading the church reconstruction project, and was a key man in creating and maintaining church morale. It was a project in which everybody was involved in some way, and that was why we had fought so hard against the state's efforts to stop it. Erno Ujvarossy had been prevented several times by the Securitate from going to the church to work on the reconstruction. When he died, they claimed it was suicide. It is true that he was suffering from depression at the time, but nobody believed it was suicide. It was as if we had been given a warning, that the authorities were prepared to use the most extreme methods to silence us and to break the spirit of our church. A reminder of this was a curious incident during a telephone conversation. My brother Istvan had managed, with some difficulty, to ring me from Canada. We talked about Erno's death. 'I don't know whether it was suicide, or—' The line went dead, and attempts to re-establish contact were fruitless.

Meanwhile, the bishop's devious plans continued as he tried to convene a Council of the Church by force. It was a scandalous abuse of episcopal power. The few members of a badly demoralised Council who gathered under duress on October 14th issued an eviction order.

I was informed of the outcome and told that I would have to leave my apartment on October 20th. I immediately appealed again and refused to leave. I announced that I was once more putting myself under voluntary house arrest. There was no legal basis for the bishop's action. The manse belonged to the church and no pastor of that church could be removed by civil courts.

The pressure upon us intensified. Uniformed and plain-clothes Securitate guards were permanently posted outside our door. I left the apartment only to conduct burials. On such occasions I took my own guards, strong young men from the church. For several weeks it was the only freedom I had – the freedom to go to the cemetery.

We were not allowed to hold presbytery meetings. The last one was broken up by the police. We were not allowed to buy food. We received anonymous threats from many sources. One telephone caller said it was a shame that the Iron Guard did not kill all the Hungarians in Transylvania in the Second World War: '. . . then he would have no Hungarian problem now.' Edit went to the market sometimes, where she was always followed. On October 28th, my father and my sixteen-year-old niece came to Temesvar. My father was to conduct our Reformation Day celebrations. They were detained at the railway station by the police and kept in custody overnight, and treated despicably.

On November 2nd, I was sitting with Edit and Mate in the small living room of our apartment which is a few yards from the front door. The door was secured with a long iron bar set on iron hooks on either side to form a strong barrier.

Suddenly there was a loud crash as the door gave way. Four masked men rushed in, brandishing knives and screaming in fury. Edit seized Mate and ran into the bedroom, pursued by two of the men. The others went for me. One slashed my forehead. Blood pouring down my face, I grabbed a chair and hit out at my attacker with it, sending the knife spinning. He fell to the floor. His partner advanced menacingly. Then our bodyguards rushed in. The attackers ran away. The whole affair had taken only a few minutes. For the whole time, Edit had shouted for help to the Securitate at our door. They made no move to help.

After that we took Mate from the kindergarten he had been attending and kept him with us in the apartment. We were frightened that more attacks might be made, and we were sure the men had intended to kill us.

I wrote to my congregation, describing the incident in full: 'I observe with bitterness that it is not so much the attackers who deserve contempt for this shameful act, but rather Laszlo Papp, bishop of Nagyvarad, and his aides who, lacking in principles, have given rise to the present situation, placing the servant of their church and its congregation at the mercy of brutal intimidation . . .'

During this time, the congregation were not allowed to bring us food, firewood or fuel. The police had confiscated my ration book, so our situation was desperate. I made an announcement from the pulpit during the Sunday service: 'I will open all the basement windows. If you would like to give us firewood, throw it into the basement.' So they did, and the same with coal. But of course the Securitate plants heard me make the announcement and sometimes they would be guarding the windows. So one person would distract the guards at one window, while others would run past, tossing fuel through the other windows as they ran.

Some brought the wood under their coats, and because they would have been searched if they had tried to bring it into our apartment, they took it upstairs to the church and put it in the small sacristy where Edit and I had first lived when we arrived. Friends did the same with food, as there was no other way they could give it to me. Soon the sacristy looked like a warehouse.

It was a terrible time, but also very moving; many of our friends and neighbours wept as they gave us their gifts. In the final Sundays before Christmas we had to move the church office up there as well, because the congregation was refused entry to the normal room and we had to make other arrangements to receive their contributions. It was as if the whole life of the church centred on that sacristy. The room that had been a symbol of Peuker's harshness and the evil power of the regime became a symbol of God's preservation in a perilous situation. Once again, God took evil and turned it to good.

On November 28th, I was told that the appeal had been turned down. My eviction was now to be enforced on December 15th. We remained in the apartment. A gang of hooligans came one night and smashed every window in the manse with beer bottles. There was no doubt that the Securitate had sent them. We sent Mate to Kolozsvar, explaining that he was going to spend Christmas with his grandparents.

In early December, my verger, Mr Mechtel, did not come to work as usual. He sent a message that he had been attacked by the Securitate and interrogated in his home. He had been forbidden to work for us. In fact, he had been told that if he set foot on the bridge over the River Bega on the way to our church, he would be thrown into the water by the police. He had tried to come by a different route, but had been followed by car and beaten up.

Christmas was fast approaching. It would have been easy to abandon the usual preparations. We were hardly in a festive mood, and the practical difficulty we were in made it almost impossible to arrange the usual Christmas activities. For example, we had three hundred children in the church, and it had become our custom to give them gifts at Christmas – cakes, apples, home-made sweets and other treats. It was a major planning operation in normal times; in these circumstances it seemed virtually unmanageable. But we were determined that our lives should be as normal as possible.

I announced that we would like people to bring to the sacristy, flour and sugar and the other ingredients for the cakes, and fruit. And we made the Christmas gifts for the children.

It was a form of passive resistance. We refused to renounce our normal lives, to give up our rights. We were determined we would, as far as possible, continue our church life just as we had before.

That was the biggest surprise for the Securitate. They were disconcerted by the reaction of our people. Even though they were stationed in our entrance, though they intimidated our people and terrorised and persecuted the leaders of the church, despite it all, the believers did not stop going to church. They did not cease to pray, to worship God, to provide Christmas gifts for the children and to continue to support their pastor. 'Preach the Word; be prepared in season and out of season,' Paul advised Timothy (2 Tim. 4:2); and the gospel was certainly bearing fruit out of season in Temesvar.

The guards at our door were not machines. Edit and I tried to treat them like human beings and to develop a relationship with them. I knew most of them to talk to. I'd say, 'Hello, why don't you allow my friend to come in? Please take a little break!' Sometimes we outwitted them. When the congregation arrived for church they were not permitted to come into the office. But when they came down after the service, I often deliberately allowed a small crowd to gather near my front door. When I had collected enough people, I opened my door and invited them to come in. There were only two guards and they could do nothing about it. Individually, most were afraid to come into the flat. Their names would have been written down, they would have been searched and afterwards they would have been harassed by the Securitate. In a group they knew they could enter.

The guards were very angry when I did this, but controlled themselves. I think they respected me to an extent; that in their hearts, they understood the rights and wrongs of the matter. Their normal manner was dour hostility. The only effective weapon against them was a kind of Christian tranquillity, a spirituality. That perplexed them because they were used to handling people who were frightened and tried to answer aggressiveness with aggressiveness.

So we approached December 15th. Romania was frequently in the world news as the systematisation programme forced villagers into housing quite inadequate for the harsh winter. We were able to receive foreign news broadcasts and knew that many people were concerned for us and for Romania. We had no idea how our own situation would end, but the nation itself seemed locked in its bleak Communism for ever.

We had some visitors even the Securitate could not notice. One was Istvan Geczy, a missionary pastor from the Reformed Church in Debrecen in Hungary. He came with gifts of food after midnight, and was able to avoid the guards. He also smuggled some money past the guards, a gift for our church from Hungarian Christians. I wrote a brief note of thanks on a tiny piece of paper, knowing that a normal letter would be found in a Securitate search. Afterwards, Istvan was stopped and searched at the border. The police searched everything, even stripping the lining from the car doors. Eventually they found the tiny piece of paper on which I had written my note. It was behind the rear mirror, tucked away almost invisibly. Later, an article appeared in the press: 'Here is your pastor who accepts your gifts of food that you can ill afford, and yet grows fat on food and money sent from abroad!'

Against the web of lies, I continued to tell the church, as I had always done, everything that had happened, often giving them the information from the pulpit. I knew that there were Securitate informers present, but I also knew that the only weapon against the lies of the regime was truth.

I composed an Advent meditation on the subject of Herod and the infant Jesus. I did not identify Herod with Ceausescu, but the analogy was clear. I wrote it on December 4th, concentrating on the oppressive, atheistic nature of Herod.

Had I known the events that were to follow, I would have dwelt much more on the profound images of deliverance and the sovereignty of God that the story of Herod's fury contains. But in early December, nobody at all contemplated the possibility that this Christmas the world might change.

8

TEMESVAR – DECEMBER 16TH

We slept badly, though thanks to the firewood we had been given we were at least warm. Edit was unable to sleep at all. Her exhaustion after so many sleepless nights was made worse by the mental strain of the day's events. I dozed fitfully in troubled snatches. Each time I woke to see Edit staring dry-eyed at nothing. By six o'clock I knew it was useless to try to sleep any more. She needed medical help.

The Securitate had not allowed our family doctor to visit for the past ten days. I decided to try to contact her. Our neighbour, Jozsef Kabai, was just going to queue for milk for his children. He promised to call the doctor.

I went to the windows and opened the shutters, shivering in the sudden cold draught. Outside, the streets were bathed in the strange half-light of very early morning: that terrible atmosphere of poverty when people stand in twilit queues for bread and milk before going to work. It was still virtually dark, but the day had begun. It was the time when one hopes it will be a good day, but knows that the hope is doomed to be crushed by the bleak realities of poverty.

I was desperately worried about Edit. I had no

idea what the consequences would be of the previous day's demonstration and lack of sleep was making me bleary-eyed and miserable. I leaned out of the window, looking down the street towards the main road, trying to see whether the situation was normal again.

Within a minute, over a dozen people had gathered beneath the window. They came from all directions, carrying shopping bags, with milk and bread. They had been watching the church, wondering if we were still inside or had been kidnapped during the night.

So began the second day.

Just as before, I talked with the people from the window. At half past eight the doctor arrived.

Dr Baranyi is a close friend of our family. She and her husband are both doctors. They are also writers who publish articles on public health and other important topics. They are in a sense missionaries among the Hungarian community, constantly helping, advising and counselling. They are much liked in Temesvar by both Hungarian and Romanian communities; in January 1990 Mr Baranyi was elected president of Temesvar. When Mrs Baranyi came into our apartment, it was a normalising influence. After ten days without medical help of any kind, we had our trusted family doctor again.

She gave Edit a thorough examination and questioned her carefully. Her expert methodical manners made us both calmer.

Half an hour after Mrs Baranyi had arrived, the mayor returned with no fewer than three doctors. He introduced them to us proudly.

'See, we have carried out our promise! We are honest men, you know. There'll be no more problems.' He beamed expansively. 'Now, these doctors must examine your wife.'

Their presence was like water to a thirsty traveller. For twenty-four hours we had been in a situation unprecedented in our experience and that of our community. Exhilarating and terrifying possibilities had opened up. The mayor and the doctors were a stabilising factor, a reminder that there was still life outside our beleaguered apartment and the thronged streets.

Mrs Baranyi remained with us until the doctors had finished. They delivered their verdict with sober faces.

'In our opinion your wife's condition is deteriorating. We consider that the life of your baby is in some danger.'

The room was warm from the wood stove, but I felt a sudden chill. I looked agonisedly at Mrs Baranyi. She shook her head angrily. The doctors continued.

'We can arrange an ambulance,' they said. 'It really is important that she be where she can be properly treated.'

The mayor contrived a look of concern. 'I am so sorry. Of course we will do everything we can to help.'

Mrs Baranyi cut in decisively. 'There is no need whatsoever for Mrs Tokes to be moved. I have examined her thoroughly myself. In *my* opinion, it would be most harmful for her to be moved.'

The argument that followed was conducted in frozen politeness. The mayor became visibly more irate, but managed to retain his mask of sympathy. The doctors used gentle words to try to persuade Edit to agree to go to the hospital. Mrs Baranyi and I encouraged her to resist. She announced that she was going to remain in our home. Eventually the mayor accepted with as good a grace as he could manage.

Shortly afterwards, workmen arrived. They were from a pool of labourers used by the regime for special tasks. We watched with amazement as they began to repair the windows.

For months glass had been prohibitively expensive in Temesvar. Even people who prided themselves on being able to manipulate the system – the kind of person who rarely had to queue, whose dinner table usually held some dainty or other from the West – could not get glass. Putty, too, was unobtainable. Now the crowd outside the door watched incredulously as glass and glazing materials were unloaded and the workmen began to repair the broken windows. Others dealt with our front door, inadequately patched up after the Securitate break-in in November; now the damage was dealt with properly. While the work was being done, a truckload of firewood arrived and was brought into our apartment. For a while, the street looked like a builder's yard.

'You see? We keep our promises,' said the mayor.

Lajos Varga: *All morning the crowd became larger. People came and went, attracted by the sight of such a large crowd and the rumour that the Securitate and the town authorities were powerless in the face of open defiance.*

There was an attempt by the police to stage the counter-demonstration ordered by the mayor the previous day, but they were forced to abandon it.

I was undecided as to how to react to these events. On one hand, I was outraged by the cynicism of what was going on. The life of my unborn baby had been used as bait to entice my wife to go to hospital. It was very clear why the suggestion had been made; the authorities wanted to separate us, to isolate me in my apartment. There was a similar cynicism behind the window repairs and the firewood. The broken windows and smashed frames of the apartment were an ugly reminder to the crowd of the persecution we had endured. While I stood at a broken window, I was the symbol and the evidence of the harshness of the regime. Mending the windows was a calculated attempt to improve its image in the eyes of the crowd.

And yet it could not be denied that the activity and the fact that things were being dealt with had a calming effect on us.

'The situation is improving,' I acknowledged to the mayor at about eleven o'clock. 'Several of our grievances have been dealt with.'

He nodded with pleasure, then pointed to the window. 'Then please, talk to the people. Tell them to leave.'

I looked out at the crowd. It was growing; the weather was bright and sunny again and it was a Saturday, so many people were in the town. Some had seen what was happening as they waited at the tramline in the main road.

They looked up expectantly. 'You have seen what has been done this morning,' I said. 'Last night we made several demands of the mayor, and this morning he has done what he promised. The situation is getting better. We've gained what we wanted. Please, go home now. It is dangerous for you to gather illegally, and besides, there is no need any more.' Their faces showed no joy. 'Thank you again, in the name of God, thank you . . .'

As soon as I had finished I realised that my plea was going to be useless. The crowd roared its disapproval, chanting in chorus, 'Don't believe him! He's a villain! Don't trust him, he is going to deceive you!'

The mayor was standing behind me. He was furious. 'Convince them!' he said angrily. I spread my hands, indicating the shouting crowd. The mayor turned and stalked out. Jeers and catcalls followed him as he pushed through the crowd to his car. At noon the repairs were all finished and the mayor returned. He was very angry. 'Are you satisfied?'

'The work is well done. Thank you.'

'Then why are all the people still here?'

I shrugged. 'I am sorry; I could not convince them.'

The mellow good-humour of the morning was gone. His anger held an open threat. 'Then you had better try again, Mr Tokes.'

I tried, but with no better success than before. Then I decided to gamble. 'Mr Mayor, come to the window with me and we will try to convince the people together.'

'It had better work,' he grunted.

But the effect on the crowd was the opposite of what he wanted. 'I am your mayor,' he shouted. 'I am giving you an assurance that Mr Tokes will not be evicted. I have the authority to promise this.'

The crowd reacted with revulsion, and some shouted accusations that I was collaborating. I defended myself as well as I could. 'What can I do?

You see the situation we are in. How will it end? The mayor has promised that everything will be all right if the demonstration ends now.'

At that stage I still believed that everything might be sorted out, that an honourable truce could be reached, that the whole episode might pass off without bloodshed. After all, our case was known in the West and Christmas was almost here. I could not imagine that the regime would try terrorist action against a known dissident during Christmas. And perhaps, after the holiday, some solution could be worked out that would allow us to continue our ministry and retain our integrity. Perhaps everything was not lost; the demonstration might have achieved, in a quite unexpected way, a lasting solution.

The crowd would have none of it. 'We want it in writing,' they demanded. 'Show us a statement! Let's see the bishop's signature!' Their spokesmen spelt out their demands to the mayor: a written assurance that I would not be evicted, a retraction of the decision to transfer me to Mineu, and a formal confirmation of my appointment as full pastor of the Temesvar church.

'In one hour,' the mayor promised. 'I will have the document in an hour.' He stormed off angrily.

It was a crucial mistake. An hour later the excuses began to arrive. It was Saturday; the offices in Bucharest were closed; nobody was available in the legal department. He might as well have poured petrol on a fire. The crowd began booing and I was not able to calm them.

At about two o'clock the deputy mayor arrived. He was a tall man in his forties with a courteous expression that very quickly altered when he saw

the mood of the crowd. 'This situation is intolerable,' he said decisively, 'and extremely dangerous.
For everybody.' He paused. 'You have one hour to
get rid of these people. If you do not, we will not
allow the situation to continue.' He stared at me
coldly. 'The matter is very well understood, Mr
Tokes.' His voice began to rise in volume. 'You do
not want to get rid of them. You organised this
demonstration. You were warned what would happen. You are responsible for *everything* that is happening here.' His voice returned to normal. 'So you
will send the people away. Do you understand me?'

He sat down and waited, arrogant in his expensive suit.

I realised that hopes of a temporary peace were
dead. The authorities were not interested in achiev-
ing a resolution of the conflict. They wanted the
crowd dispersed, and after that, I had no doubt
reprisals would follow. I felt a sense of failure; the
crowd outside the window included many of my
congregation and many from neighbouring
churches, maintaining vigil as protest at my
eviction; now, it seemed, no peaceful conclusion
was possible.

'I am simply unable to send them away,' I said
dully. 'I have tried without success.'

'Then try again, Mr Tokes.'

An idea came to me. 'Ask the leaders of all the
churches in the town to come here. The mayor can
make his promise and they will witness it. If a
written document is impossible, the people will
probably accept that as a guarantee.'

The deputy mayor reached for the telephone. I
began to explain that it was not working, that it
had been disconnected by the authorities after my

Panorama broadcast; and that when our home was broken into by armed thugs we had been unable to telephone for help.

Before I could finish my sentence he was dialling. In seconds he was talking to the mayor. It seemed that at some point in the afternoon the telephone had been reconnected.

The conversation was short and unproductive. 'The suggestion is not acceptable,' said the deputy mayor, replacing the telephone firmly.

I thought hard. 'Then ask a delegation from the street to come in here,' I suggested. 'The whole situation can be talked through and we can agree some kind of end to the demonstration.' The deputy mayor considered the suggestion. 'Go and tell them,' he said.

Half an hour later, six Romanians and four Hungarians sat down at the long table in the church office. The discussion began. The deputy mayor was charming and considerate, but it was clear that nobody trusted him, and the debate was angry and inconclusive. Eventually the deputy mayor phoned the mayor to report what progress had so far been achieved. He promised that within an hour a document would be ready, that it would be faxed from Bucharest. Representatives of our congregation would be able to collect it in an hour from the town hall. I did not ask why Bucharest was suddenly able to produce documents on a Saturday.

During the period of waiting, the tension outside was increased by people in the crowd systematically trying to aggravate matters. One roughly dressed man was shouting continuously. 'Let's break into the house. The Securitate are in there; they're trying to kidnap Laszlo Tokes! Let's rush them!'

I shouted back, 'It isn't true, I am here with the deputy mayor and some friends. Don't you understand what that man is? He's a provocateur, he is trying to get you into trouble. Don't listen to him. Don't let him influence you.' After ten minutes, the man left.

When the hour was up, Mr Sepsi, a leading figure in our congregation, went with two others to the town hall. But, of course, there was no document, and he returned empty-handed.

Now there was no longer any pretence at negotiation. The mayor sent back a curt message that if the crowd had not dispersed by five o'clock, the fire brigade would be sent in to disperse them by water cannon. That was his ultimatum, and I knew then that the matter would end in tragedy.

The dominant obsession of the crowd outside the church that afternoon was that the Securitate were in our apartment, either holding us against our will or preparing to abduct us. It was a fear incited by provocateurs in the crowd, who could be seen clearly directing people's emotions. There was a core in the crowd composed of people who had come to join the vigil against the eviction, but most had come because they had seen the disturbance while out in the city or had heard about what was happening at the church. Some had no idea what had started the demonstration. All day people came and went; as some left to go to their homes or to queue for food, others arrived to take their place. Consequently I had to go to the windows frequently to assure new arrivals that I was still alive and had not been evicted.

My pleas to them no longer concerned the promises the mayor had made and apparently fulfilled. 'Go home,' I said. 'They will use force, the Securitate will come back; the mayor has made it quite clear. What power have we against them? Only tragedy can come out of this.'

But the crowd's resolve only hardened. 'We want Tokes! We love you, we won't let you be taken away!' Some forced their way into the hallway and almost broke down the door; we heard the fighting between my guards and the people who wanted to come in.

Our feelings were in turmoil. The pace of events was bewildering, and the cumulative effect of each new ultimatum was creating unbearable tension in Edit and myself. Every half-hour I had to go to the window and repeat the same explanations and make the same appeals. There was a rising hysteria in the crowd that was having its effect on me. I felt as if I had lost my bearings, that I had no way of orientating myself in the claustrophobia of the flat. Desperately worried about Edit, helpless to resolve the crisis developing outside, I thought I was going mad. Though the crowd looked to me as a figurehead, in truth I was a prisoner of their anger.

I was torn between two desires: as a Christian pastor I wanted to protect them from the violence which I was sure was inevitable, and at the same time I wanted to stand with them in their protests against the regime's illegality. Like Moses who accepted the role given him by God to stand up against an oppressive regime, I believed it was my duty to stand with the crowd.

I had spent the afternoon in that conflict. By six o'clock I had resigned myself to whatever might happen.

A few people in the crowd shouted up to me: 'Come down into the street and lead us!' Others took up the idea, and soon there were dozens of people chanting appeals to me to lead them to the city centre for a mass demonstration. I refused. Partly it was because I wanted to be a pastor and not a political crusader, partly because I could see in the crowd people I knew to be Securitate officers, and I was alarmed at the obvious provocation from individuals in the crowd clearly intent on making the situation uncontrollable.

Later, thinking about the events of those two days, I realised that the authorities would have had a great deal to gain if the situation had become a riot. It would then have been possible to subdue it by force and put the entire blame on the Hungarian community. It would be a perfect excuse for even heavier oppression of Hungarians and all minorities.

By seven o'clock our friends reported that the crowd now stretched from the church down to the Opera Square several blocks away, where many people were gathered on the steps of the Orthodox church. Now there were two crowds in one.

Lajos Varga: *As on the previous night, the people had lit candles and some were singing hymns. There were Securitate officers in the crowd, observing, but they could do very little. Round the church, people joined hands in a human chain of symbolic defence.*

Laszlo Tokes appeared from time to time, and people begged him to conduct a service. He was too exhausted to do so, but he spoke briefly to us from the Bible, for only a few minutes at a time.

And then, about half past seven, among the shouting and the excitement, the unimaginable happened. From a number of places in the crowd the first notes of a prohibited Romanian song rose quietly into the night. Awake, Romania, *which had not been sung in public during Ceausescu's reign, faltered bravely on the lips of people who could barely remember the words.*

The song was an intensely nationalist one and un-known in the Hungarian community. I looked out of the window and was moved by the sight and sound of Romanians singing. It was a striking token that this was a demonstration not just by our minority church, but by the whole population of Temesvar.

I did not know the words of *Awake, Romania* and did not know how to respond. In the end I placed my hand over my heart as if a national anthem were being sung and listened quietly.

It would have been impossible to sing in any case. My throat was so sore that I could hardly speak. I had been calling down to the crowd every half-hour all day. But it was a solemn time of communion between us.

And then the crowd was shouting new and danger-ous words; from the main road to the Opera Square, voices were crying, 'Down with Ceausescu! Down with the regime! Down with Communism!'

The situation changed irrevocably at that point. The crowd did not want to hear me any more. Nothing I had to say could shift the burning focus of their anger now. I closed the window and went to join Edit and our friends.

Arpad Gazda, member of the church and friend of Laszlo Tokes: *On the previous evening I had been one of those who had gone into Laszlo Tokes's apartment with the Party secretary.*

The next morning I went back to the apartment and was allowed to go in. I was with Laszlo and his wife all day. Other friends came as well. By the evening there were nine of us in the apartment: Laszlo, his wife Edit, her brother-in-law Pali, myself, a fifty-year old parishoner and four other friends of the Tokes family.

We were very frightened. We had no idea how the matter was going to be resolved or how long the authorities would permit the demonstration to go on. But we knew we were in great danger.

'The crowd's moving!'

Our guards at the door came in with the news that the people had begun to move off. The demands for me to come to the window stopped. We looked out without being seen and watched the numbers in the side street diminishing as people moved over the bridge towards the centre. In the main road, the trams had long since stopped running. The stationary vehicles formed a natural barricade, creating a line of defence in front of the church building. After a short time, the side street was virtually empty. Only a core of church members and friends remained to keep their vigil.

One image from that night will stay with me for ever. The Securitate and militia became increasingly active in the street as the number of people diminished. One young demonstrator was standing near the window. I did not know who he was. He was arguing with Securitate officers. Suddenly they began punching him and beating him with sticks. He fell to the ground. They kicked him, viciously and expertly. He was covered in blood, and unconscious long before they stopped their attack. His body remained motionless on the ground in front of our window for a long time before it was dragged away. He seemed to be dead.

Lajos Varga: *The crowd divided. The largest part, including the students, headed for the city centre. They arrived at the Party headquarters in the mood for violence. They began by breaking all the windows.*

Just before ten o'clock at night, police reinforcements arrived. They succeeded in breaking up that demonstration and forced the demonstrators back to Laszlo Tokes's church where they turned water cannons on them. By then I had left the church demonstration to go home to my wife. I told her, 'This isn't a demonstration any more. This is a revolution.'

Later I was told what had happened next. The crowd seized the water cannon machine, broke it up and threw the pieces into the Bega River. This was an extraordinary achievement as the machine was supposedly virtually indestructible. More violence followed; they smashed shop windows; they broke into a bookshop, seized all of Ceausescu's books and burned them.

At the church, there was no more violence at our doors and the Securitate did nothing. We could only wait and pray.

I do not know what happened in the centre of Temesvar that night or how many demonstrators remained there. The fighting we could see from our windows lasted for several hours. We were appalled and terrified.

From our windows on the main road we could

hear the noise of windows breaking and fires starting. We saw the water cannon being brought out. Civil and uniformed militia appeared at the far end of the side street, sweeping people ahead of them into the main road, but the crowds there forced them to retreat. At that time we heard no shooting.

Lajos Varga: *During the rest of the evening the protests elsewhere in the city grew more extreme. The police in their turn became violent, but the demonstrators only became more violent themselves.*

Looking for symbols of the regime to attack, they found a shop selling fur coats and expensive garments – the kind of clothes that only the Securitate and Nomenklatura could afford. They broke into the shop and set it on fire.

At midnight there was relative silence. The soldiers, militia and Securitate agents had left the street. The fighting was far from the church. Hardly anybody was about in the streets. Occasionally a vehicle went by; usually a ghost-like military vehicle, ominously armoured, bound for the site of the riots. There was an unreal, phantom atmosphere. We sat together in one room. Sometimes one of us would go to the window for a few minutes, returning to tell any news.

We set out the long office table for supper. There was some foreign food in the cupboards that we had been keeping for a special occasion. We put it on the table. We took special care arranging the meal, wanting it to be as beautiful as we could make it. Then we sat down together, all nine of us, full of suppressed excitement but outwardly calm.

As we ate, we talked about the events of the past two days and tried to draw some conclusions.

We felt that if Bucharest followed the example of Temesvar, we could be saved.

Talk became desultory. We were each occupied with our own thoughts, fears and spiritual reflections. Our conversation was like a series of monologues. At the same time, we were prepared like a condemned person is prepared for execution. We were convinced that an attack would come shortly.

At one o'clock we decided it was time to sleep. We had passed most of the evening in a companionable silence. The atmosphere was one of reconciliation, of forgiveness, of the kind when farewells are taken of people you know you may not meet again. It was a profoundly Christian atmosphere; we were truly one in spirit. For us, it was in a most profound way, our Last Supper.

We said good night to each other. Edit and I said goodbye to our friends. We agreed that one or two would stand guard all night and the others would go to bed. I needed to prepare a sermon for the next day; it had been agreed with the crowd earlier that we would have morning worship in the church as usual next morning.

On my way to bed I packed some essentials into plastic bags, added the church funds (kept in cash: they would have been seized if we had banked them), and put the bags near the door so that if we were attacked in the night we could take them as we escaped. Then I went into the courtyard in the centre of the building and listened. In the distance I thought I could hear sporadic gunfire from the direction of the university.

At three o'clock in the morning, Pali came into our bedroom.

'We're under attack,' he said. His voice was distorted with tension.

It took three or four minutes for the attackers to break through the iron bar that secured our front door. In that time we grabbed what clothes we could, seized the plastic bags and locked the interior doors of the apartment to gain a few precious seconds as the Securitate smashed each one to get to us. I had no time to find my shoes and left my bedroom wearing a pair of yellow fabric slippers.

Our plan was to withdraw to the church upstairs by climbing the outside wall. In the courtyard we found the ladder we had concealed previously and put it up against the windows of the church.

It was a bitterly cold night. We had to climb a distance of about eight metres. The ladder was narrow and unstable. As we prepared to climb we saw plain-clothes Securitate men forcing their way into the courtyard. I went first with Edit, carrying the bags. Pali and Arpad Gazda followed. For a few heart-stopping minutes I helped my pregnant wife climb precariously up into the gloom. When we were safely up, the first Securitate men were in the courtyard below. 'Pull the ladder up!' shouted one of our friends. 'We'll go back inside!'

It is amazing how many thoughts can race through your mind in a brief moment. I was aware of the danger to my friends below, and did not want to abandon them. But I realised that the main anger of the authorities was directed at me and I was grateful that we were safe. The issue was decided for me as I heard the others barricading themselves into the apartment below. Quickly we hauled the ladder up. We were like medieval warriors in a besieged fortress. *The church has always been under siege*, I reflected sadly. *All our churches in Romania have been encircled by Communism, by the Dictator's power. We have to resist or die. We are committed now.*

The church was in darkness. We fumbled for a switch. Edit sat down, obviously in pain. I could hear her gasping for breath. 'We're in the church,' I said to her gently. 'We're in sanctuary. Perhaps they won't break into the church.' Arpad went to the back of the church and found the switch. As the light came on, the Securitate hammered on the locked door.

I opened the sacristy, the small room where Edit and I had been forced to live when we first came to Temesvar. I calculated that barricading ourselves inside it would gain us five or ten minutes. It was useless. Nothing could stop our arrest now. Better to face them in the church, with dignity and faith.

Everything was happening much too quickly. I could not think what I should be saying to the others, what my responsibilities as a pastor were in this situation. My heavy clerical vestment was hanging in the sacristy. I wrapped it round my shoulders; there was no time to put it on properly. I picked up a Bible and held it like a weapon.

We were standing round the Communion table. The door gave way with a great crash. An enormous number of plain-clothes and uniformed men erupted into the room. We stood and faced them, I wrapped in my full clerical robe and wearing the ridiculous yellow slippers.

It took seconds for them to surround and separate us. Arpad was the first to be arrested. He was punched and kicked. I saw Edit surrounded by officers, seized roughly and taken away; they were careful not to hit her. She and Pali were on one side of the Communion table, I was on the other. I lost sight of them in the confusion. A uniformed Securitate officer, Veverka, stood in front of me. He was about fifty, a large powerful man; I know his name because after the Revolution he was imprisoned and tried in Temesvar. He smashed a white-gloved fist into my stomach.

I was beaten up brutally and expertly. One blow to my face drove my teeth through my lip, another started my nose bleeding. Soon my face was covered in blood. They searched me roughly. Now I was expecting the worst. There was every possibility that we would be shot there in the church.

I was dragged down to my office. On the way Veverka was still punching me in the face.

'You are to blame,' he said over and over again. 'It is your fault. We'll show you the God of the Hungarians. And then we'll kill you. You see, you've no chance.' He swore, hurling filth and profanities at me, mocking my helplessness. I made no reply.

Waiting in my office, now crowded with police, militia and Securitate, were the Party secretary I had seen the previous Wednesday and a prominent official from Bucharest: Cumpanasu, Head of the Department of Cults. Veverka pushed me through the door. The rain of blows continued. Cumpanasu's face wrinkled in distaste. 'Please – don't beat him so, please stop now.'

I looked at him through a bloody mist. He looked back as if he did not know who I was. The punches stopped. I was led to my own desk.

'Sign this paper.'

'What is it?'

'Your acceptance of your dismissal and eviction.'

I groped for the paper and tried to focus.

'There's nothing on it. It's blank.'

'That doesn't concern you. It will be dealt with later. Sign.'

I refused and received another punch. Eventually I signed. The paper was taken from me and carefully put away. There was a veneer of formality about the proceedings. One of the people in the office was a lawyer in charge of evictions, and a form of official procedure was being precariously observed. The fact that I was bleeding profusely and wearing a clerical robe and yellow slippers made the whole scene surreal. I asked if I could put my shoes on, but was refused.

I could not see Edit, but I knew she was in another part of the office. She had asked for a glass of water to take her medicine, but the request was refused. I had no doubt that we would be separated now. Where the others were, I had no idea.

Eventually I was taken into the street. It was like a scene from a war film. Only a few street lamps were lit, making a patchwork of shadows. The street was full of vehicles – many cars, an ambulance, an army car and a militia wagon. People in uniform were everywhere. My neighbours were looking out of their windows, attracted by the noise. The officers shouted at them to close their shutters. On the far side of the main road I could see shops with their windows smashed.

I was pushed into the back seat of an official car with uniformed militia on either side of me. As I got in I saw Edit being pushed into another. She was crying for help. 'Laszlo! Laszlo!'

They forced her into the car also between two

militia. The cars moved off. When I saw both were travelling in the same direction, I felt a flicker of hope.

Nobody said anything to me. I sat immobile, blood still trickling from my mouth and nose. I decided that my last act of resistance would be that I would neither move nor speak. That was all that was left to express my anger.

The cars travelled through streets that bore the marks of fierce fighting and eventually arrived at the Securitate headquarters.

9

THE ROAD TO MINEU

The courtyard of the Securitate headquarters looked like an old engraving of the gates of Hell. It was in almost total darkness; the only light came from the doors and windows of the building. Cars roared in and out at great speed, and soldiers were running in all directions at the command of officers who appeared from the main building shouting orders. It was like a scene at Gestapo headquarters in a war film, with the same kind of hysterical fury. People were standing in isolated groups; some were weeping. At the front of the building, partly covered, was a row of dead bodies. Dead bodies were everywhere.

The two cars stopped in the courtyard. I memorised the number of the car that Edit was in so that I would know it again. I stared, horrified, at the scenes in the courtyard, but my guards pushed my head down so that I could no longer see. The officer in the front of the car got out and went into the headquarters building. He was gone ten minutes, which I spent with my head between my knees. At last he returned, said something to the driver, and the cars swung out of the entrance and back on to the road.

Nobody said anything to me. I had no idea where we were going. It seemed to me we were on our last journey to execution. I imagined we would be taken before a firing squad, or they would use a method we had often heard about – the condemned person was taken to the frontier and thrown out of the car. As he ran to freedom, he was gunned down by his guards.

At the same time, a small hope still flickered. Our cars were travelling together. At least we were not being separated further. Perhaps the publicity my case had received in the West had had an effect. Perhaps even the regime hesitated before attacking a pregnant woman.

Meanwhile I sat silent and impassive, though I was taking in every detail of the route we were taking. Five cars set out from the headquarters northwards in the direction of Arad. There were soldiers everywhere and a military observation post at every crossroads. From Arad we sped north again to Nagyvarad, then took the eastern road towards Kolozsvar. At every county border a new car was waiting, and men with radio telephones were directed by senior county officials. It was like being the baton in a relay race. Intermittent rain through the night sometimes soaked our clothes as we changed cars.

The sun rose as we drove on, but it was a dawn of great sadness such as might break on the last hours of a defeated army. Yet in those hours I regained my spiritual strength. I had time to collect my thoughts and think calmly about all that had happened. I was in physical pain from the savage beating I had received. My lip was throbbing, my face was bruised, and the cold fear was beginning to settle in

my mind that Edit might lose our baby. But sand-
wiched between the two guards I was alone with
God and my thoughts, and as we hurtled towards
Kolozsvar my peace of mind returned.

We were travelling east. To the south-east,
beyond the mountains, lay the capital, Bucharest.
Ceausescu's grand strategy for dealing with the
Hungarian problem called for the forced resettlement of Transylvanians in the east. Perhaps that
was where we were going. Or perhaps we were
heading due east to Moldavia, or to a remote district
near the Soviet border far from anybody who knew
us and what we had fought for. They had tried
to silence us by sending us to Temesvar; now
they would bury us deep in the Old Kingdom, as
effectively as if we had been executed.

But fifty kilometres from Kolozsvar, the cars
turned left, heading north again into the Salaj
district.

It is difficult to communicate the feelings I experienced then. First, I was sure I knew where we were
going. I knew the road well; it plunged into the
beautiful mountains that rise west of Kolozsvar.
There is only one significant town on that road –
Simleu-Silvaniei. Less than twenty kilometres
further on the road emerges near Zalau on the main
road to Satu-Mare. But we were not going to Satu-
Mare. In a valley not far from Zalau lies the tiny
village of Mineu.

I was still sitting stony-faced between my captors,
but inside I was gripped by a singing joy. It was not
only because I now knew that we were not to be
executed, that the authorities were simply im-
plementing Bishop Papp's decree of exile. It was
much more, for the countryside of Salaj has a

significance for me and Edit that anybody born outside Transylvania will find hard to understand fully.

The familiar villages and churches of Salaj dominate the landscape of my childhood. It is the landscape celebrated by the poet, Ady, one of its most famous sons. As a young man I loved Ady's poems, and explored the region with his lines singing in my mind; today his poetry still has a special resonance for me, for it evokes the beauty of Salaj.

The people of that region are as enduring as their land. They are warm-hearted, kindly people, whose destiny is wedded to the soil from which they make their living.

In the Bible God tells us that we are made from dust; the land is part of us. As the cars travelled over the rough roads of Salaj, I knew I was coming home. The realisation made my eyes fill with tears, for the first time in that night of fear and pain.

At the border of Salaj we again changed cars, but this time there was an unexplained delay. We waited. Nobody told us what was happening. Now that the cars were stationary, I was cold. Without socks, the yellow slippers gave no warmth to my feet, and I shivered in my black suit.

After an hour a truck arrived to join the convoy and the cars drove on.

The procession of vehicles came to a halt at last in the village that was part of the commune to which Mineu belonged. A guard opened the car door and motioned me to get out. I emerged stiff and sore, my body reminding me of the beating I had received that night. As I took my first tentative steps, my yellow-slippered feet squelched in thick mud. The entire village was an ocean of mud, and soon my trouserlegs were caked.

In the commune building a tall, slender man and a Romanian woman waited. 'You are now pastor in this commune,' the man informed me. 'I have to tell you that we do not tolerate illegal activities. You will be expected to cooperate with the mayor,' he said. 'Your role here is to be obedient. We want your best efforts, Mr Tokes.'

His attitude and that of his companion veered bewilderingly between harsh authority and sympathetic gentleness. The woman tried to cheer me up. 'You should try to smile,' she urged. 'You'll feel better if you smile.'

I pointed at my battered face. 'Can't you see? I'm covered in blood.' I had said very little since leaving Temesvar and speaking was painful with my punctured lip.

She brought water in a small bowl. Touching my face was agony; my lip was badly swollen and my nose felt tender, but I managed to get the worst of the caked blood off. The act of washing made me feel more normal, more human. Suddenly I realised what I must look like – a six-foot prisoner, bruised and scarred, wearing a muddy suit of clerical black and a pair of ruined slippers. The thought forced a smile to my lips. The woman nodded approvingly. 'Now you rejoin your wife,' she said.

I was ushered out into the muddy road again. The place was swarming with officials from the other cars. Their presence lent an air of respectability to the occasion; they were actors in the pantomime of sham legal niceties that had been going on all night. No villagers were to be seen. Behind the curtained and shuttered windows, I knew people were watching what was happening. I wondered what they thought of the new pastor of Mineu.

Edit and I were put into the back seat of a new car. We looked at each other with great happiness, but did not dare to embrace or even hold hands or say anything to each other for fear of punishment.

At midday, at the end of a lonely rough track that went nowhere else, we arrived in Mineu. The cars slipped and skidded up a muddy lane and stopped outside a small church building and an old wooden church tower. There were soldiers waiting for us. They had radios and had obviously been in contact with the convoy as it travelled from Temesvar.

We got out of the car. Most of the people of Mineu were in church, but some were waiting to meet us. Edit and I looked for the first time at our new parishioners.

Like most villagers in Ceausescu's Romania, the people of Mineu had an oppressed, beaten look. Years of toil and the demands of the regime, even in that remote place, had stamped their mark on the faces of those who stood waiting to greet us. Some had tears of sympathy in their eyes as they looked at us, our clothes still damp from the rain in the night, Edit grey and worn from the journey, me with streaks of blood still on my bruised and swollen face.

The dean, Mr Ady, headed the reception committee. He had, we learned later, been woken in the early hours of the morning and told to prepare the manse for our arrival. It had been unoccupied for several years, and the dean had been able to do little more than light the fires and sweep some of the dust and cobwebs away.

He greeted me formally on behalf of the church and handed me a document. I glanced at it briefly, too tired and confused to read it properly. It seemed to be our official assignment to Mineu. As I tried to make sense of the paper, the large truck that had joined us at Arad was opened up. Men were summoned from the church to help carry the contents into the manse. The truck had been loaded with our possessions, seized randomly from the apartment.

We went into the manse. The early afternoon sun revealed the dust on the walls, and evidence of mice and other vermin was everywhere. Edit groaned and looked even more miserable as men dumped boxes of our clothes and items of furniture in the cold rooms.

The guards spelt out the terms of our enforced occupation of the manse. From now on, I would be allowed to leave the manse only to take church services. The one person from the village who was to be allowed to speak with us was Mr Ady, but he would be permitted to see us only if guards were also present. Food would be brought to our door by people from the village, and if we needed anything we were to ask them, but only in the presence of the guards.

The formalities over, we were finally allowed to begin to settle into our new home. Women from the village took away the worst of our garments to wash. We arranged some of the furniture half-heartedly. Outside in the garden of the manse, soldiers were boarding up the gates and the gaps in the hedge. Soon a barrier like a prison fence had been erected all round the house and garden. The guards stationed themselves around the house. It was like Temesvar all over again, except now we were in an abandoned building in which the cold seemed to have soaked permanently into the walls.

Edit's heroic patience finally ran out. She collapsed, weeping uncontrollably. Now, after hours of travel and separation from her by ominous guards, I was able to hold her in my arms. But she couldn't be comforted. She was in a world of her own, dominated by fear for the baby she was carrying and the trauma of the events of the past forty-eight hours.

We struggled through the remainder of the afternoon. I unpacked a few of the boxes and sorted out some of our possessions. They had been snatched up carelessly with no attempt to protect them from damage or to pack them properly.

To my astonishment I discovered our radio among the confusion – whether brought by accident or because we were intended to hear the government's propaganda messages I never discovered. But that night we listened to foreign broadcasts. Hungarian news, Radio Free Europe, Voice of America, foreign news stations – all beginning to broadcast the first fragments of the story. Something had happened in Temesvar – there had been a major demonstration, people had died, the roads in and out of the city were closed. It was as much as we ourselves knew of what had happened. But one fact gave us the beginnings of hope. We had said in our apartment in Temesvar as we ate our last meal, that if the demonstrations reached Bucharest, there was hope. From the radio reports, it seemed that the fighting was continuing and the world was on our side.

At about seven o'clock we were allowed two visitors. They were both Hungarians, members of the ruling board of the commune. They tried to comfort us.

'It's not so bad here. People in this village are very kind. Everybody wants to do all they can to make you feel at home. Please don't give up hope.'

Afterwards I wondered whether they had come spontaneously or whether they had been sent by the authorities to try to bring me to a more docile frame of mind. But questions like that were too burdensome for the end of such a day.

We had no idea what would happen the next day. Our bodies were aching and our minds exhausted. Edit had long since passed the limits of her endurance and was now in uncharted depths of mental and physical strain. But we were alive and we were together, and we were still in our beloved Transylvania.

Edit went to bed first. I stayed up a little longer, looking out of the window at the lane outside. After the clamour of the past two nights, Mineu was blissfully silent, its peace broken only by restless poultry and the movements of the soldiers. I eased my aching body out of my clothes, placed my Bible by my bedside and prepared myself for sleep. My last act before getting into bed was to take off the yellow slippers.

10

THE DARKEST HOUR AND
THE DAWN

The next morning we woke to the sound of frenzied activity in the village. Ducks and geese protested loudly as army vehicles carrying new guards roared into the village; the watch was changed about every eight hours. From the window, we saw peasants going by, and the Orthodox priest. Nobody was allowed contact with us. We learned later that all the villagers had been visited by the Securitate and warned not to have anything to do with us.

We were brought food three times a day, and the villagers contributed. But we were only allowed food if the head of the village was present. His name was Aaron Ankel, a very good man, who was close to tears when he was with us.

Our main concern was that our families should know we were safe. But none of the radio reports said we were in Mineu. Later we heard that a huge crowd gathered at the church in Temesvar on the Sunday and the street was closed off by two buses. The militia told them we had run away. The deputy bishop came to Temesvar on Saturday evening intending to preach at my church the next morning, but by then the Revolution had begun and he had to go back to Nagyvarad.

In Mineu, we had no telephone, and we did not want to burden Aaron Ankel further by asking him to take messages, for he was under surveillance too. We prayed that somehow the villagers would get the news to our families, and so in fact they did.

Monday was the first day of Holy Week. A large truck arrived, and men began to install electric equipment round the building. When they had finished we found that strong electric lamps had been set all round the manse, like floodlights round a concentration camp, and soldiers with dogs were patrolling the grounds. We were trapped in a fortified house, completely helpless in the hands of our persecutors.

I was told my first sermon in Mineu was to be given at eight o'clock that morning. As I made my way to the church between soldiers and tracker dogs, I felt weak and my body ached. Bathing and shaving had been excruciating. I opened the church Bible virtually at random. Somehow I managed to preach a sermon, but I felt as if I was preaching from the depths of a deep pit of depression. 'Out of the depths I cry to you,' wrote the psalmist, and I identified with his misery.

Edit was in bed, ill. The guards offered to take her to the doctor in the city, but we refused. We were afraid it was a trick to separate us, like the one that had been tried in Temesvar, and we wanted above everything to be together.

On Tuesday December 19th, they began to interrogate us. We had to wake up at six and were then taken to Zalau. We saw as we left Mineu that a roadblock had been set up, and everybody wanting to enter the village was being questioned.

I was interrogated in the military headquarters and Edit in the medical headquarters. Her interrogators were men. The interrogation teams were hand-picked; one from Bucharest, another from Moldavia, others also were drafted in from various parts of Romania.

They demanded a reconstruction of the events of the last weeks. They had a list of all those who had visited us. I was ordered to write lengthy statements. During three days I wrote fifty or sixty pages, and my handwriting is unusually small. The statements had to be in Romanian. My grasp of that language improved very much that week, and I felt the benefit when, after the Revolution, I preached to Romanian congregations.

The interrogators used a wide variety of techniques. Mostly they tried to intimidate us. Their leader from Bucharest warned me: 'I could beat you until you died.' Then, with a look of vicious contempt: 'But – I have no wish to soil my hands with Hungarian blood.' With Edit, they used the classic technique of alternating abusive shouting with apparent sympathy. Sometimes they tried to confuse us with lies. I was told that Edit had admitted that I was in the pay of foreign citizens, that Gazda had confessed that we were trying to raise a rebel army to fight for Transylvanian independence.

The interrogation was relentless. We were given no time to think how to answer. They were trying to make us confess we were in league with foreign powers. Our friends had already confessed, they said. Now *we* must make a public confession.

They tried hard to project an intellectual image.

One bragged of his expertise in psychology and history, sociology and demography. While I was writing out my statement, he sat reading a Romanian translation of a bestselling book by a well-known American writer.

I quickly realised that in interrogation the battle is a mental one. There is a psychology of interrogation. For most of the time we had no idea what they planned to do with us, even from day to day. I felt like the object of a scientific experiment. For example, they made it clear each morning when we left Mineu that we might not be sleeping there that night. So we never knew what was happening. It was frustrating and wearying.

But I, too, had my own psychology. As a Christian I believe that every time we come into contact with a human being, it is of immense significance. We have to take our fellow human beings extremely seriously. So I tried to behave towards the Securitate just as I would behave with anybody else. Sometimes, when they were adopting the 'soft' approach, it was possible to have a rational conversation with them.

'I'm not demanding that you be a Christian,' I said. 'I am only asking you to be a human being. And then you must acknowledge that you know the realities of this situation. You know what is going on.' I wanted to make an impression on their spiritual consciences, to touch them at that level so that they would go on thinking about what I had said long after we had gone. I did not despise them. I took them seriously as human beings.

The interrogation went on for three days. We arrived back at our prison in Mineu each evening exhausted. Most of our time there was spent listening to the radio, trying to piece together the sequence of events that had taken place in Temesvar since our departure and then in Arad, Nagyvarad and elsewhere. We drew strength from the support expressed for us from many sources.

On the second day, Edit was feeling particularly unwell, but was taken off to interrogation just the same. I was edgy all day, sometimes refusing to answer further questions until I had been given assurances that Edit was all right; twice they had been forced to take me to see her before I would continue. It was a small but determined act of peaceful resistance.

At about four o'clock, I asked again how she was.

'You should be happy now,' said my inquisitor. 'She's been taken back to Mineu.'

'Why? Has her condition become worse?'

The guard was almost jovial. 'No! Don't worry! We finished our business with her today.' He returned to his notes. 'Now, let us continue.'

After three hours, the interrogation stopped. My guard took my sheaves of statements from me. 'Now,' he said, still in an affable voice, 'we listen to the radio.'

They arranged the room like an auditorium. Chairs were placed in formal rows in front of a radio set and I was made to sit down. The Securitate sat around me. There was an almost carnival atmosphere. 'The Conducator will speak,' they said, giving Ceausescu the title he most enjoyed. Ceausescu had returned that day from a visit to Iran, one of Romania's few allies. Now he was to broadcast about the events that had occurred during his absence.

He addressed the entire country, and almost his first words were about Temesvar. 'Everything that happened in Temesvar started at a church,' he said, 'with the case of a priest who was legally served notice to quit and refused.' He warned that Romania's borders were at risk from a revolutionary movement that had started from abroad with foreign money.

As I sat with the men who were listening to their idol, a single fact reverberated in my mind. If you were mentioned in a speech by the Conducator, and you were the focus of his analysis, it meant that you were going to be executed.

In a moment I saw the whole masterly plan. Edit and I, and our friends being interrogated in Temesvar, were going to be the scapegoats. Everything that had happened would be interpreted as an anti-revolutionary act by the Hungarians and their foreign partners. It was even possible that Ceausescu intended to use the events to unleash a wave of anti-Hungarian feeling against all Hungarians in Romania, so that the final solution to his Hungarian problem would be achieved.

There would be a show trial in front of the entire television audience. The result would be a foregone conclusion.

I was devastated. I knew now that there can be a point in a man's life when he can resist no further, when suicide begins to seem a reasonable choice. The Securitate were watching me openly during the broadcast, taking a sadistic pleasure in my reactions.

After the speech they put their strongest pressure

on me to admit that I was a spy and had organised
the Temesvar revolution.

'If you don't admit it you can never go back to
Mineu,' they assured me. 'You will never see your
wife again. We can spare your life only if you admit
that you are the sole organiser, the chief rebel.'

But to my surprise, I was taken back home just
before midnight. I was reunited with Edit, but we
spent a miserable night. A Securitate officer had sat
with her and made her listen to the broadcast as
well, and the effect on her had been the same as
upon me. Our time together that night was a kind of
farewell, because we had no idea what would happen the next day. We did not sleep very much. I
listened to the radio until three o'clock, hunting for
news.

The next day in Bucharest, Ceausescu appeared
at a carefully staged pro-government rally. A crowd
of 100,000 had been ordered to applaud and give a
demonstration of loyalty for the benefit of the millions watching on television. But instead of a
crushing triumph, the television audience saw the
first crumbling of the dictator's hold on his people.
Voices from the crowd shouted 'Murderer!' and
'Timisoara (Temesvar)!'

Ceausescu looked old and bewildered. An expression of bleak distaste appeared on the face of his
wife, Elena – a face already etched in lines of cruelty.
Ceausescu's announcements of pay increases,
grants to pregnant women and other inducements
to calm made no difference to the crowd's anger.
Soon the couple were forced to go indoors.

The borders were still closed and foreign news
agencies had little information. When we listened to
the news that night after our interrogation, the

historic events of the day were only sketchily known. We did not know the scale of the slaughter or the extent of the unrest. We did not know that there was a massacre in my own city of Kolozsvar or that the massacre in Temesvar had been one of unprecedented ferocity. But we knew that the Revolution was spreading, and that people all over the world were praying for us.

During Thursday, our neighbours from across the lane, Jeno and Margit Varga, who had attempted to visit us several times, were finally allowed to see us for five minutes. They brought a gift of food: a pair of sausages, cooked for us by Margit.

Next morning the interrogators failed to appear to take us to Zalau. We listened to the morning news. The situation was critical. Rebellion was every-where. The West had issued statements, sent obser-vers and generally made protests. Many people had expressed support for us.

With every hour that passed without the appear-ance of the Securitate, we gained hope. But it was mixed with uncertainty. The police were still outside the fence; we were still imprisoned.

Just before noon, army jeeps pulled up outside the manse. To our astonishment, the guards were ordered into the vehicles and driven away. Our prison had been abandoned.

We did nothing immediately; we were too fright-ened. We began to listen to every sound and analyse every movement. A little later, we heard a car coming towards the church. My heart was in my mouth. Perhaps this was the moment; perhaps we were to be taken to Bucharest for the show trial. It was a black Russian Volga, a model the Securitate used.

Our joy was inexpressible when out of the car stepped my wife's uncle and my father-in-law. They were our first visitors. The very fact that they had been allowed to come was a good sign. They brought news that people everywhere were rising up, that something was going to happen. They said they had been stopped in Zalau and told they could visit us for an hour, and then take us back there. We were astonished that such a relaxed arrangement had been made after the harshness of our treatment during the week.

We were joyful together. I think, after the sorrow and fear of the previous evenings, it was one of the happiest days of my life. They stayed with us for more than an hour and we were late leaving for Zalau. But before we left we listened to the one o'clock news. And that was when we heard that Ceausescu was on the run.

Our immediate reaction was of disbelief; then came the realisation that now we did not have to go to Zalau. But a kind of reflex ingrained in us during the past week made us obey, and we returned with our relatives. I presented myself at the Securitate headquarters. The interrogators were subdued. They shook hands with us and told us very politely that we were now free to go.

We got back to Mineu, to a scene of ecstatic happiness. The whole village was in the church. The villagers came to us one by one, all weeping and rejoicing with us. Within an hour, people poured into Mineu through the mountains, by car, by wagon, by tractor. The manse was surrounded by people shouting, 'Long live Laszlo Tokes!'

Suddenly it was a feast day, like one of the great Church festivals. All afternoon people came with food and wine, bringing gifts, taking photographs of exuberant groups. The radio gave hourly news bulletins and every hour people insisted I should preach a sermon.

I preached several times before nightfall. The church was constantly full of people giving thanks. I preached from the sixteenth chapter of Isaiah, which speaks of the fall of tyrants and the day of the Lord's blessing. At one point I was preaching in the churchyard because the church was overflowing. The worship continued. For four days, it was like a continual thanksgiving service.

The media began to arrive on the Friday we were released; we were deluged by reporters, cameramen and interviewers. At three o'clock Jeno and Margit Varga invited us to move into their home, where they had a comfortable room. We were very grateful for two reasons. One was that the manse was now permanently besieged by reporters and there was no peace for Edit, who was still recovering. The other reason, which was the best possible Christmas present that we could have had, was that two days later, on Christmas Eve, my parents brought Mate to Mineu.

In the midst of the euphoria, there was still fear. As we sat and watched the television news and saw the face of Nicolae Ceausescu, we felt the charismatic strength of his presence in an uncanny way. He had been so much a part of our everyday life. Now he was gone from his place.

It was then that violence began to erupt all over the country. For two days Ceausescu was on the run, and nobody knew where he was. We were afraid that terrorists would come to Mineu, or that the local Securitate would make it their base for a last-ditch stand. And we could not shake off a dreadful fear that Ceausescu himself might come. We began to look around in alarm when anybody entered the room.

When we heard he had been captured, the news was part of the joy of Christmas. I revised my material on Herod and the infant Jesus that I had written earlier, and preached on the subject. Now the application was very easy to make.

Herod was a picture of Ceausescu who threatened the life of Jesus, the life of his people. The fall of Herod was a parallel to the fall of Ceausescu. The relationship between the two seemed very real.

All the events of the Christmas story now had a new, brilliant dimension for us, a dimension of history rooted in the reality of our lives. It was something very beautiful and very profound to be meditating on those eternal truths and seeing them echoed in our own immediate history. For those of us who lived through them, the days of Christmas 1989 represented a rich, resonant embroidery of the Christmas story, a time when the providence of God and the foolishness of human wickedness seemed as easy to comprehend as the sun and the moon over the timeless Transylvanian hills.

11

NEW BEGINNINGS

Mineu is a peaceful village set in gentle slopes among the mountains north of Kolozsvar. Its isolation is emphasised by the poor roads that lead there – their surfaces either rutted and bumpy or with large holes roughly filled with loads of gravel. There is a village shop in Mineu, selling everything from huge circular loaves of bread to warm, hand-knitted pullovers; and along each of its lanes, flocks of poultry wander noisily.

The people of Mineu have an uncomplicated generosity. When we first arrived in the police car, exhausted, beaten and in despair, they stood round us, their eyes eloquent with sympathy. Though they had all been warned that we were dangerous dissidents with whom they were to have nothing to do, they tried to help in many ways. After the fall of Ceausescu, when the Securitate had gone, we learned for the first time how many of them had tried to visit us with gifts and offers of help and been turned away at the gate.

They were a community like the people I had known as a young man in Szentmarton, or in the villages I had visited with Janos Herman, the elderly pastor I had so much admired. Years of oppression

had left their mark on the people of Mineu. There
was fear in their eyes, a hunted look, when the
Securitate controlled their village. But even when
there were more Securitate in the village than had
ever visited it before, they retained an underlying
fierce independence that nothing could destroy.

Mineu was a village in which, had God called me
to be pastor there, I would have gladly spent my life,
seeking out the people of God and being their
spiritual shepherd. I was in a strange situation, I
realised, as the excitement gave way to a future
without shape and full of possibilities. I *was* the
pastor of these people. I had a piece of paper to
prove it, drawn up by a bishop of the Church.

But it was not God's appointment. It was an
expedient, a way of getting rid of me. If I had
accepted the appointment to Mineu, I would have
been collaborating with the regime in suppressing
the truth and opposing the Holy Spirit.

Mineu was a haven of peace and beauty for us
after the brutality and horror of the previous week.
We were loved and protected by the villagers. After
living with the threat of violence for most of his
young life, Mate was free to wander the lanes of
Mineu as much as he liked, greeted as he went by
scores of new friends.

We knew we could not remain in Mineu for ever.
Our Temesvar congregation and a different
Romania were waiting for our return. But before
that came Christmas.

For the first time in four decades, Christmas was
declared a public holiday. All over Romania, there
was rejoicing as people who had for years been
denied the right to practise their faith openly took to

the streets in acts of worship and celebration. Priests and pastors who had carried out their duties in fear of harassment or worse punishment now addressed large crowds. In cities all over the country, the people of Romania knelt, prayed and wept for joy.

Romania was suddenly the focus of the world's Christmas. After the few days in which the borders were closed and hardly any news leaked out to the outside world, the country was now open again, more open than it had been for years. Visitors thronged in. Hungarians came who previously had been unable to visit without great difficulty and lengthy border formalities. People from neighbouring Eastern European countries who had already received their freedom in the astonishing events of that autumn came. And the world's press came too, many of them making the journey to Mineu to interview and film us.

The whole community of Mineu took on the task of caring for us during these days. Our neighbours, Jeno and Margit Varga, cared for us as members of their own family. They were unimpressed by the most prestigious visiting cards and insisted on our privacy when they considered we needed to rest. I preached many sermons and gave many interviews.

All over the country, people who had been kept away from the centres of power and privilege now broke into the Party offices and Ceausescu's numerous homes and looked with awe and hatred at the stupendous extravagance with which the regime and its leaders had surrounded themselves. In Temesvar, my friend Lajos Varga showed foreign journalists round the villa kept in permanent readiness for Ceausescu should he decide to make one of his almost unheard-of appearances in the city. He took great delight in using the dictator's bathroom and stretching himself out luxuriously on the dictator's bed. In the Romania that had existed until only a week before, it had been forbidden to walk on the pavement that ran past the building.

The collapse of the Ceausescus seemed total. Nicolae and Elena were in prison, seized after attempting to leave the country; they tried unsuccessfully to bribe their captors. Nicu, their son, whose boorish behaviour and manic personality were notorious well beyond the Transylvanian region of Sibiu over which he ruled as Party leader, was arrested there. Filmed for the world to see, bruised and humiliated, he was a visual symbol of the fall of the dynasty.

And yet the malevolent aura of the Ceausescus still had power to make people fear. There were rumours that the main water supplies in Temesvar and Sibiu had been poisoned, that in their madness Nicolae and Elena had planned a final catastrophe to bring their whole doomed country down with them in flames. There were fears that Securitate forces still holding out in Bucharest were planning a rescue attempt, perhaps through the vast network of tunnels with which they had honeycombed the city to facilitate just such an operation. Later, when film of the trial was examined, some people pointed out Ceausescu's frequent glances at his watch and said there was an escape plot actually in operation and that the watch contained some kind of transmitter to give the signal to the Securitate waiting nearby. It may or may not have been true, but it indicates the mystique that surrounded the pair.

Later, prevention of a rescue attempt and further

bloodshed was the main reason given by the interim government for the decision it took some time between Thursday, December 21st when he was arrested, and Monday, December 25th. A sombre spokesman appeared on television on Christmas Day and announced the summary trial and execution of Nicolae and Elena Ceausescu.

In the Vargas' home, Margit, standing by the window, turned on the radio and heard the news.

'Mummy,' demanded her small daughter, 'why are you crying?'

'Because Communism is over,' she replied.

The execution of the dictator had seemed unthinkable, and the news came as a devastating shock to many who had dreamed of such an event for years. But the brief numbing horror soon gave way to rejoicing. The official television announcement by Petre Popescu, detailing six counts on which the Ceausescus had been found guilty, was followed by others less formal. A radio announcer called it 'wonderful news . . . the Antichrist has died'; a weather forecaster declared, 'On 25 December in Romania, there is Spring.'

For myself, I found the pair more ridiculous than hateful. Of course, in one sense they represented Antichrist. But their speeches and megalomania seemed dangerously ludicrous. In many ways, Elena was the stronger and more forceful of the two; she was Nicolae's destiny. But neither was greater than any other human being. I found it hard to take their extravagances seriously. They were little people, full of sins, needing to be saved by God.

Photographs of their corpses were published in the newspapers and shown on television. After all the brutality and corruption, the persecution and the murder, now they had no rank, no position; they were pitiful peasants, stripped of all that they ever did or owned. In truth, my response as I looked at them, staring in death, was one of pity.

On December 24th, another political development appeared in the newspaper. The newly created National Salvation Front announced its Council. Among the names was my own. Nobody had invited me to take part, and the announcement came as a complete surprise to me.

It was an odd experience to see myself listed with a number of people who had served under Ceausescu. Many well-known dissidents were also on the list; some of them were believers. Doina Cornea's name was included, for example. An Eastern-Rite Catholic, she had written a number of extremely courageous open letters that were highly critical of the government. For that she was imprisoned and tortured. In 1988 the British ambassador had been arrested as he tried to visit her.

It was a very great honour to be on the list, though one I accepted with mixed feelings. I hoped that those who were now governing the country wanted democratic as well as revolutionary change.

Invitations were already flooding in for me to preach in churches all over Romania. On Boxing Day I delivered my first sermon outside Mineu – in Zalau, where I had recently been taken for interrogation. There we were welcomed by the pastor who, among other kindnesses, gave us the luxury of our first shower since leaving Temesvar. Pastor Molnar had been a wonderful support to us since our release, often visiting us two or three times a day, bringing medicine for Mate, dresses for Edit and much more.

When we arrived in Zalau I realised for the first time what a phenomenon my name and our congregation's struggle in Temesvar had become. The streets round the church were thronged with people. When the time came for me to preach, the church, which holds 1,500 people, was full, and the service had to be relayed to the crowd outside.

In my sermon I returned to the book of Isaiah and spoke about the overthrow of dictators, God's sovereignty in history and the need for people everywhere on this day of great rejoicing to repent and turn to God.

On December 27th, I travelled to Bucharest for the initial meetings of the new Council. It was a sobering experience to see the devastation caused by the fighting. Buildings were destroyed, streets littered with rubble and broken glass, tanks and soldiers everywhere. I realised Temesvar must also look like that now – rubbled streets and squares around the church, where thousands of my fellow citizens had died.

It was a joy to meet others who had fought against the regime, and to be reminded that God had used many people from many backgrounds.

In the discussions I asked a question: How had the Ceausescus been buried?

Ion Iliescu was visibly angry that I should be concerned at all about their fate. I was saddened by his response. I had not questioned the execution, merely expressed an interest as a human being in the way the Ceausescus' remains were disposed of. I was ashamed that I should be embarrassed to raise such a question there.

For most of January I travelled round Romania
preaching many sermons. My texts were often
taken from Isaiah, and the themes I chose were the
ones that had occupied my mind since the Revolution: the wonder at what God had done in our
country, and the need for us to respond to it personally rather than just be swept along in a wave of
euphoria.

The Hungarian Reformed Church was changing,
just as the whole country was changing. The two
bishops were gone; Gyula Nagy had been visited by
a small group of believers and persuaded to resign,
and Laszlo Papp had disappeared from Nagyvarad
in Christmas week. On the day of Ceausescu's
flight, a statement by him appeared in the newspapers tracing the whole of the troubles to me. I was, he
asserted, a troublemaker, rebelling against the discipline of the Church, providing biased interpretations to the outside world. A few days later he
himself fled the country, ousted by the people of
Nagyvarad. As this book goes to press, six months
after these events, you can still see the word 'Judas'
painted on the wall of the bishop's palace in Nagyvarad. In the Theological Institute at Kolozsvar, the
walls are lined with photographs of past students
and the Church hierarchy. Wherever Laszlo Papp's
picture appears, the students have pasted a black
mourning stripe on his lapel – the acknowledgment
normally given to one who is dead.

I was elated that my persecutor had gone, that the
priesthood of God was now free of one who had
served it badly. But I was grieved, too, that the
person who had presented a carefully slanted version of the events in Temesvar was my own bishop.
The charge of being a traitor and a troublemaker

came not from Romanian nationalists, nor from Communists, nor from the Securitate. It was Laszlo Papp's choice to give the misinformation to the people.

And that was Ceausescu's way: he turned Hungarians against themselves. To justify his illegalities and the actions of his regime against Hungarians, he found in Papp a willing Hungarian ready to serve him.

In Nagyvarad, virtually the entire staff of the bishop's office resigned, even typists and secretaries. Prominent among those who urged them to go was my friend from college days, Pastor Attila Veres-Kovacs. In Kolozsvar, the Revolution was only partial. There are church office-holders in the diocese today who were puppets of the old regime.

At the end of January, we returned to Temesvar. It was a poignant return. During our absence, thousands had been killed in the bitter fighting. Buildings were burned-out shells, and everywhere there were the same reminders of the fighting that had been visible in Bucharest. But there were joyful reunions with our friends, those with whom we had shared the frightening, wonderful days of December.

The first service we held was an ecumenical one. I remembered the support we had had from other believers during our months of suffering and during the final demonstration, and it was a joy to welcome members of several other Temesvar congregations to our celebration.

What happened in our church in December was not merely a minority victory. It was an event which we shared with all Romania. In the crowds around the church there had been Protestants and Catholics, Hungarians and Romanians. We wanted them with us for the thanksgiving too, and we wanted to take their hands in friendship as we set out together on the next phase of our national life.

Sadly, not all of our homecoming was joyful. Since the death of Ceausescu, anonymous threats had been made against me, some of them death threats. For many months now we had been used to such messages and knew they stemmed from the Securitate. Now we wondered whether members of the Securitate still at large were seeking vengeance. In the past, too, we had had threats from Romanian nationalists. Perhaps the new messages came from them. Whatever their source, they were worrying. Since leaving Mineu, we had been given armed protection. Now security around us was tightened.

Since early January, plans had been made for me to speak in foreign countries. At the beginning of February I began a two-week visit to Hungary. Before that I went to see Ion Iliescu.

'I am going to be speaking in Hungary, and later in America. There will be other countries, too. As a member of the provisional government I want to represent Romania. What is your advice? How should I speak? Of course I want to represent all our people. I do not go as a Hungarian but as a Romanian.'

'Of course.' Iliescu was charming and noncommittal. He held out his hand. 'Well, have a good journey.'

It was becoming clear that the dissidents who had been invited to join the Council were not there to discuss the real problems of the country. They were a shop window of the Revolution, appointed to legitimise it. Here are the dissidents, here are the minorities, the Front seemed to be saying to the world. Romania is set on a good path.

One by one, the dissidents became disenchanted and left. I made several statements in January expressing dissatisfaction with the interim government's apparent unwillingness to make a radical break with many of the old regime's structures. By the time I came back from my foreign travels, my links with the Council of the Front for National Salvation no longer existed.

Outside the stadium in Budapest, coaches arrived from Romania bringing peasants in their traditional working clothes. Inside, the huge auditorium held an audience remarkable for the fact that Hungarians and Romanians were sitting together. The plan for the evening included two addresses by myself and a packed programme of song, music and poetry. The audience sat enraptured as much by the haunting beauty of a Romanian folk song as by a fine performance of a piece by the Hungarian, Erkel. When I spoke, I spoke in Hungarian and Romanian.

Throughout the evening, the two cultures intertwined. It was a deeply moving occasion for me, for it brought together so many of the chief concerns of my life: music and literature, the opportunity to speak to people about God, and a visible demonstration of reconciliation. During the evening a child movingly recited a poem about resurrection. On an occasion such as this, it was possible to glimpse a reborn future.

In two respects the evening was typical of the whole of the trip. First, it was televised; behind the speaker's platform and the artiste's podium, an enormous electronic screen displayed the picture that millions were receiving on their television sets at home. Secondly, the security was extremely strict. I was surrounded by police and security guards, and few were allowed backstage.

The publicity and the security were both exhausting. Edit and Mate came with me to Hungary, but we had little free time. On one day in the small town of Berekfurdo, I had to fit a haircut into a schedule that had had to be revised early in the morning when several unexpected visitors from Church and press arrived. At the Theological Academy in Debrecen, where I received an honorary doctorate, the corridor leading to the room in which we sat was lined with security guards and academy staff who were instructed to let nobody through without a search.

Such a way of life is exciting and exhilarating for approximately twenty-four hours; then it becomes very tiring. Edit, especially, who was now in the second half of her pregnancy, found it difficult. But we were also moved by the love and affection we received everywhere. Many people asked me to sign their Bibles and prayer books. It was a new experience for me, and took much longer than I had expected, as I always added a biblical reference or spiritual encouragement.

The trip was organised by Istvan Geczy (who had visited us in Temesvar) and his friend Attila Kocsis, on behalf of the Reformed Ministers' Alliance of Hungary. They arranged my preaching tour around seven cities, and meetings with the Prime Minister, the Foreign Minister and other leading political figures and ecclesiastical dignitaries. A meeting was also arranged with Cardinal Casarolli of the Vatican, and I was received by the British Ambassador at his residence.

The great gala in Budapest was organised separately, by Dezso Abraham, a businessman from Budapest who has become a close friend of my family and our church and has played a major part in my foreign tours.

After a brief return to Temesvar, we set out again, this time for America and Canada. When we left, Romania was tense. Following the heady joy of the Revolution, many disturbing developments were taking place.

It was becoming clear that our Revolution itself had been at best a partial one. Those whose hopes at Christmas had been so strong, hopes of a government in which all minorities would have their voice, were resigned to the reality that after Ceausescu, it was going to take a long time for democracy in any broad sense to appear. Many individuals and parties representing minorities were no longer part of the Council.

The practicalities of government, too, demanded that at least some of those in government had to be people who had to some extent been part of the old regime. There had been no political opposition in Romania; the only politicians were Communists. And the only people who had basic information on the day-to-day executive tasks of government were the people who had done the job before. Ion Iliescu had left Ceausescu's government some years before, but in the minds of many he was still associated with it, and there was widespread unease at his use of many of the old methods.

The marginalisation of minorities in the pro-

visional government was reflected in Romanian
society. After long years of deprivation, it was now
possible for Hungarians to have some of the rights
that had been denied them, chiefly in education and
literature. But at the same time, Romanian nationalism often strongly opposed moves forward, a restoration of Hungarian rights. During my visit to
America, the tensions flared up into violence in the
city of Tirgu-Mures.

The trouble centred around the celebration, on
March 15th, of the anniversary of the Hungarian
Revolution of 1848. Both Hungarian and Romanian
feelings were running high. There was a car accident, the exact cause of which was disputed,
resulting in death and injuries with many people
involved. Soon there was a major demonstration
that turned into a riot. Among many anti-Hungarian slogans, some shouted 'Death to Tokes!',
and the same words were painted on shop
windows. By nightfall, the city was under martial
law and the roads were sealed. In Tirgu-Mures, a
curfew was in force. Tanks patrolled streets littered
with debris. In one of the squares, the burned-out
shell of a bus lay on its side. At the municipal
hospital, the staff were tending the wounded.

The tension continued for days.

A major factor in the conflict was the role of
the Romanian nationalist organisation, Vatra
Romaneasca. Under the mask of a cultural organisation, this is a fiercely nationalist movement with an
agenda comparable to the Iron Guard of the 1940s
and Ceausescu's Securitate. It draws its inspiration
from Daco-Romanian ideology, which claims that
Romanians are the direct descendants of the
Romans, and have held 'Greater Romania' (which

extends into the Soviet Union to the east and into the whole of present-day Hungary to the west) since the earliest times. It is a theory at best, and has little support from academics and historians outside Romania.

The propaganda of Vatra recalls in some ways that of Hitler against the Jews. They say that Hungarians are a contamination of pure Romania; that they must be purged from the country; that the same goes for Jews, Gypsies and all ethnic minorities. In March, they claimed a membership of seven million Romanians.

They were the chief provocateurs of the March fighting. They planned to create an anti-Hungarian movement that would spread throughout Transylvania, with Tirgu-Mures as its epicentre. Their main strategy was to exploit what was a very real problem in the university. Under Ceausescu, the university had been forced to adopt Romanian as its teaching language. As the university was a Hungarian foundation, this caused great hardship to existing and potential Hungarian students. Now that the Revolution had happened, there were calls for the university to revert to being Hungarian-speaking.

It was an understandable demand, at a time when many injustices were being put right. But it would have meant that Romanian students would have been in exactly the same situation as the Hungarians had been. While I do not believe that it would be impossible to work out a solution acceptable to everybody, it is not the kind of issue that can be resolved by taking to the streets. But for an organisation like Vatra, it was a wonderful opportunity to inflame prejudice and anger.

In America and Canada, I spoke to politicians of all parties, to small groups, and to churches. I had talks with President Bush and with the Prime Minister of Canada.

My message was always the same.

First, I described the events in Temesvar and the Revolution that had followed. In this I was an ambassador of our Revolution, a messenger of the changes taking place in our society. I was able to tell them that when the tyrant had seemed immovable, when it seemed that nothing would ever change in Romania, when many of us had given up hope, change took place.

Secondly I was a messenger of reconciliation. I was able to tell of the way in which, during our Revolution, people had worked together who had previously been afraid and suspicious of each other. I told of the ecumenical initiatives our church had taken. I told them of others throughout Romania who were working for reconciliation. I told them that at Christmas one of our first acts was to have a joint service with the Orthodox Church in Mineu.

I spoke of the Church's role, for I wanted not just to describe reconciliation, but to be its servant. To that end, I made use of the credit of the gospel and of the Church; I claimed the right to speak about reconciliation because I was a Christian minister.

In the past, the clerics of my church used the credit of the gospel to spread misinformation. Now it was time to use the weapon of the gospel as it was meant to be used.

Thirdly, I wanted to serve the interests of my country, Romania. I did not go to America as a Transylvanian separatist or an anti-Romanian nationalist, for I am neither of those things. I accept from God the reality of the Transylvanian borders as they now exist. I care for the Romanian people. I had no wish to stand in America as the representative of a problem minority, making a case for myself against the majority of the people of the country in which I make my home.

Yet, at the same time, I wanted to serve the cause of the freedom of religion and also that of the rights of minorities in a mixed society.

In my speeches and talks in America I tried to make a synthesis of all these concerns. I believe I succeeded. The American press made no distinction between 'ethnic Romanian' and 'ethnic Hungarian' when they wrote about me. I was simply a Romanian pastor. Nothing in my speeches or discussions caused them to do otherwise.

I believe, in fact, that I did more for my country than anybody else did in America during that month, because we had no other ambassadors for reconciliation and the American government had not yet initiated talks with the Iliescu government.

So it was a great sadness to me when I returned home to find my visit caricatured and exaggerated claims made about what I had actually said. For example, I was widely reported as having commented on the Most Favoured Nation status of Romania. I did make a statement about it. I said that in Ceausescu's time, MFN status meant that the government benefited and the people got nothing. I counselled careful monitoring of the Iliescu government's performance.

It was interpreted in Romania as an anti-Romania speech. It was not. It was an anti-government speech, sceptical of all governments. In any case, I had no brief from the government. Ion Iliescu had specifically declined my offer to speak on its behalf. I was a private citizen, in America, with a right to a political opinion. Even some Christians were critical of me for having that.

When I returned from America I went direct to Bucharest. Ion Iliescu gave me permission to address the parliament. I spoke of the events in Tirgu-Mures. I said that the Hungarians were prepared for reconciliation and the claims that we were secessionist and anti-Romanian were mere propaganda. I identified the problem of reconciliation as a problem on the road to democratisation that could not be bypassed.

'This is not only a problem for two million Hungarians,' I said. 'It is a problem that affects the entire population of Romania. Those who work to prevent reconciliation are fighting against democracy.'

I sat down to total silence. Nobody applauded or made any other sign of acceptance. The parliament was normally a noisy place; the silence was uncanny and threatening.

As business moved on and the level of hubbub rose again, I reflected that the small political prestige I had acquired from my role in December was rapidly running out.

During the same trip I spoke in Geneva, at the invitation of the Central Committee of the World Council of Churches. I knew that it was an opportunity to speak plainly, and I made the best use of it I could.

I told them of the disappointment our church felt that there had been so few expressions of concern from Western churches, until the very last days of the Ceausescu regime. I pointed out our own church's past involvement with the anti-apartheid movement in South Africa; there had been no corresponding commitment to the situation of our minority church. The World Council of Churches, like most Western Christian bodies, had allowed itself to be deceived by lies.

'The Romanian Church authorities, opportunist and collaborating bishops and preachers of ecumenism, succeeded in misleading their sister churches and the public opinion of the ecumenical movement abroad in exactly the same way that the Ceausescu regime deceived the international community,' I declared; and so the protests from the West that would undoubtedly have influenced church freedoms in my country never came. In the past few years, I pointed out, Laszlo Papp's voice had commanded more respect in the World Council of Churches than mine.

I challenged the Council to 'break free from the strait-jackets of ecumenical diplomacy', and urged future support for the churches in Romania. My speech was received graciously, and the Central Committee affirmed its commitment to Eastern Europe and its sorrow for mistakes made in the past.

Since the forced resignations of the two bishops and the prospect of the first properly constituted episcopal elections for decades, my name had been put forward as bishop. It was a very strange feeling, having had such a difficult relationship with both Papp and Nagy, and there was some opposition. Eventually I was nominated and elected to the bishopric of Nagyvarad. I was deeply moved. Since my days at the Theological Institute, I had desired to play a part in the leadership of the Church, to rebuild the strong fortress of God from the inside. Now I was to do so. My friend Attila Veres-Kovacs was also elected as deputy bishop. We shared a common vision, and we had a task to do that we relished.

My installation as bishop took place in Nagyvarad on May 8th. It was a joyous, festive occasion. In my address (included as the last chapter of this book), I charted a new course. It was one in which we were all united. I announced the motto that I would take for my bishopric: 'With God for the people.'

A fortnight later, Romania held its first free elections. Predictably, the National Salvation Front led by Ion Iliescu won a large majority – two-thirds of the vote. The Democratic Alliance of Hungarians in Romania took second place with less than ten per cent. I had stood as a candidate for the Senate, standing as an Alliance candidate. I was defeated.

The defeat was a harsh disappointment. I had stood for election in Temesvar. There was some evidence of electoral malpractice, but the message in Temesvar seemed to be the same as in Romania as a whole; the Revolution had only partially penetrated our society. There was not yet a massive popular demand for a rejection of Communism. Had the elections been run with total integrity and propriety, Iliescu would still have been victorious, and the result in Temesvar may well have been the same. Democracy, in its fullest sense, lies in the future for our country.

And so as we look to the future, Romania's course is uncertain. There are tensions that will not be easily resolved. On June 14th, an anti-Communist demonstration in Bucharest was ruthlessly put down by miners, called in to the city by the Iliescu government with instructions to deal with the problem by force. The result was many wounded, intimidation and violence against minority parties and their leaders, and attacks on opposition newspapers and publishing houses that effectively closed down the opposition voice for a time. Among the miners were several known Securitate. At the time, I was in Paris. I sent a telegram of protest to Iliescu, stating that I could no longer support the government and warning of the danger of civil war.

The activities of Vatra Romaneasca and other nationalists grow more extreme. Petrol was poured under my brother Andras' front door, and windows were broken in my sister's home. A warning issued in June declared that on August 15th, every Hungarian in Romania would be driven naked back to Budapest.

The question that is often asked in the West is: Will there be civil war or a second Revolution in Romania? And my response is: I hope there will not be civil war and I hope there will be a second Revolution.

For we need a second revolution. It will not be a revolution such as we experienced in December 1989. It will come about, I hope, because Romania becomes part of the international community and establishes links with international movements and institutions. The desire for democracy in the international community is so strong and the changes taking place in Eastern Europe so powerful, that Romania cannot, I trust and pray, avoid its second revolution.

I hope it will be a non-violent revolution, fertilised by the democratic ideals of Eastern Europe and the democratic West.

To facilitate this, freedom of information, access to the means of communication, modern technology, equipment and resources are crucial factors. Those who resist the second revolution fear these things. In Bucharest in the June demonstrations, the anger of the miners extended to technical equipment, printing machines, fax machines and computers. They destroyed the equipment of publishing houses of the opposition press. This emphasises the close link between modern technology and democracy.

That is one considerable way in which we can benefit from our new, open relationship with the technological West. But I hope that we will have the wisdom to use the West's gifts discerningly. Often Western technology has created a Western human alienation. I hope we will be able to avoid that, and perhaps our long cultural tradition will help us to resist being overcome by the novelty and power of the technology we need.

But as I look at the West, with its mixture of the good and the bad, my fear is that we will find ourselves in a colonial situation. Having extricated ourselves from dependence on the Soviet bloc, it is possible now to fall into the arms of the materialism of the West.

It is here that the churches can make a major contribution. They still have an influence in Romania and their structures survive. I hope they will find a role in preserving our national heritage, and that they will accept it before the situation is irredeemable.

I have enjoyed my visits to the West greatly and have been much impressed by the technological society. Yet at the heart of it I sense a deep impersonality. Romanians find the overorganised life strange. For example, in America I had to use elevators all the time. Soon I longed for a flight of stairs!

And yet the chief distinction between our society and Western society is that Western society *functions*. Ours does not. Even if you are rich and own many beautiful properties and have many possessions, none of them works properly. It is a defect in our society, caused by the fact that Communism destroyed the old structures of society and had no idea how to build new ones. The village systematisation policy was a symbol of this. What we need for the future is a society that functions, but is built on spiritual values. In the dawn of a new Romania, I feel myself to be living in the ruins of an old society.

In the bishop's office in Nagyvarad, we have opened our doors. We have limited the powers of the bishop, and we have tried to break down the old walls between the clergy and the people. There is laughter and conversation in our office, and visitors are made welcome.

Wherever we can, we are striving for reconciliation, a bringing of people together. Our Hungarian church is developing links with other churches. We are building a new church in Temesvar, for the use of Protestants and Roman Catholics; on the steeple there will be the Reformation star, and on the front door will be a cross. It is an ecumenical symbol of the

Revolution. For forty years, there was no Catholic bishop at Nagyvarad. Now there is, and we are looking forward to working together in many ways.

We are looking, too, for ways in which our church can help other minorities; for example, in preparing and distributing Bibles and Christian literature for the gypsy community in their own language.

It may seem naive or overoptimistic, in the light of some aspects of present-day Romania, to fight for reconciliation. But I can see no other perspective in which to fight. Even if we do not succeed, there is no other cause worth fighting for.

And that is why spiritual values must lie at the heart of our new society. If any power or any force can achieve reconciliation, it is the Christian faith. Our faith is the most universal ideology that we possess. Those of us who are believers must learn that it is in trust in God, through the strength our faith gives us, that all our life together, our future, our survival and our joy as a nation lies.

BISHOP LASZLO TOKES

Installation Address

Nagyvarad, May 8th, 1990

With God, for the People

'I have redeemed you; I have called you by name; you are mine' (Isa. 43:1).

My first act as bishop of the Reformed Church District of Kiralyhago is to thank God for his honouring mercy. I also thank the people of our congregation for their confidence in me. My vocation, and the fact that the councils of the Protestant congregation have elected me, compel me to take up this responsibility as my duty, and to devote the best of my abilities and understanding to the service of the glory of God and the Church.

As I enter my new service, I remember with respect my grandparents, who as 'the servants of the nation' preached the word of God as pastors and teachers of the people. They took care of the needy in the land of Transylvania, in Malnas and Szentmarton.

From the bottom of my heart I thank my parents, who carried on their shoulders the task of caring for a numerous family, guided us on the path of God and also taught us to serve our greater family, the

Church and the people. In the 'congregation' of my seven brothers, they gave us a model of humanity and courage.

I am moved in my heart as I remember the world of the struggling people of the Transylvanian Plateau, my predestined 'native land'. Within that world I remember Szepkenyeruszentmarton. This small village represented for me the most complete Reformed congregation and Hungarian community. Their destiny was for me the most compelling demonstration of the realities of our minority church. They showed me the way of the self-sacrificing Jesus Christ.

With thanksgiving I remember the places where I served as a clergyman: Brasso, the mission congregation from Zernyest, Dej and Szasznyires. These were my 'schools', teaching me love and a commitment to community.

I pay homage to Temesvar and to the congregation at Temesvar, singled out by history; and to the village of Menyo in Szilagysag, whose people reminded us of the evangelical dignity of those 'little ones' of Jesus Christ.

God and the people were always one in my life.

Now, following the way of life of forefathers, of families, and congregations, of clergymen and of the destiny of my native land, I come to Transylvania: the country of silent church bells and the dead sea.

I entered Kiralyhago travelling to the Partium on the historical route taken by the great prince and ruler Gabor Bethlen, and by the 'Guardian of the Bible' Gyorgy Rakoczi, who during the siege of Nagyvarad saved the half-burnt Bible for the people who thirsted for the word of God. And so we also thirst; that is what justifies our being together today, seeking the true way of liberation, seeking our future, seeking a better and more pleasant life for our people who live in a national struggle. 'Surely God is my salvation; I will trust and not be afraid. The Lord, the Lord, is my strength . . . With joy you will draw water from the wells of salvation' (Isa. 12:2–3).

So I could formulate my motto as pastor up to this moment as this: 'With God for the People'.

This is the idea according to which my wife and I live. This idea brought about the revolutionary events in Temesvar. This kind of thinking will guide me during my future work.

The Sources of Rebirth

Remember your leaders, who spoke the word of God to you. Consider the outcome of their way of life and imitate their faith (Heb. 13:7).

The 1990th year of God begins a new chapter in the life of the Reformed Church District of Kiralyhago county. The new leading body of our Church is taking over its task at a time when our society has experienced revolutionary transformation. Leaving behind us what was perhaps the darkest period of our history, our new circumstances offer the unique possibility of a religious rebirth, and oblige us to act.

These circumstances are doubly relevant to us, for God has used our Church for the liberation of our country; just as he once sent David to fight a giant, so he sent our congregation at Temesvar to fight against the Goliath of dictatorship.

We can think about our Church's rebirth in the context of two important anniversaries.

Seventy years ago, as a result of the Treaty of Trianon, our Church seceded from the Hungarian Church district over the Tisza and declared itself an independent church district. Istvan Sulyok, pastor in the new area of Nagyvarad, Dean of Bihar County, the charismatic leader of our Church and its first bishop, took up a historic mission when he built a new church on the ruins. With tireless labour and with the help of colleagues who also deserve praise, he built a highway in the desert.

Now, in our new age of historical and social changes, the same task awaits us: the rebuilding of the threatened Church. Revival, now as ever, is vital for our very existence.

Our source of strength for the revival of our Church could be symbolised by another anniversary, one with broad historical reverberations. The Bible of Gaspar Karolyi of Vizsoly is now four hundred years old. Our new-but-ancient church district can be proud of the fact that it gave Hungarians the author of the most significant Hungarian literary work of the sixteenth century, who was born in Nagykaroly. The Partium bestowed our people with the living Gospel, and included in the rights it established that of our 'sweet mother language'. Gaspar Karolyi – 'the man who conquers without wounding' – could well become the symbol of 'the noble fight' of our Church revival.

Yes! We need now the living and communicating gospel of the Holy Scriptures to prevent the perishing of the flock that is once again growing, to pour faith and hope into those who are discouraged. Let us lead those who are thirsty to the wonderful cool waters of faith, and build a strong foundation for the future.

The Reformation was founded on the rediscovering of the gospel. If we too return to the gospel, we may count on developing progressive reformational traditions. When we return to the gospel, we are inspired from clear sources. The principle of continuous reformation – 'semper reformari' – tells us this. The gospel is a clear spring emerging from the rock in the desert; it is a power that will hold us secure for a thousand years.

Let *this* year be an anniversary year. Let it be the year when sermons were revived in our churches. Let us once again put the Holy Scriptures in their appropriate place. Let our Church be strengthened from the universal festivity of the Holy Bible, and let it search the Holy Scriptures for its future service.

The Church is our Powerful Fortress

Your people will rebuild the ancient ruins and will raise up the age-old foundations; you will be called Repairer of Broken Walls, Restorer of Streets with Dwellings (Isa. 58:12).

1. 'God is a mighty fortress', Martin Luther's hymn tells us. We may paraphrase the famous line to form one of the great realities of the Christian life: 'The Church is our powerful fortress'.

Let us consider the abiding strength of the Church, the eternity which is given physical shape in centuries-old walls, architectural styles that speak of eternity, strongly built towers. And in that context, let us consider the historical and social role of the Church and the force of teaching, traditions and system of values, that give people a spirit of community. Let us then consider the place occupied in our world of thinking and emotions by the Holy Spirit, and on the earthly presence of the Church as the body of our Christ.

In all times the Church has been our strongest refuge: a spring of consolation and hope, a survival shelter and an eternal harbour.

Just as once upon a time Jerusalem was besieged by the conquerors of Zion, so was our Church besieged by the dictatorship in an attempt to separate us from our last refuge, our faith. It was an attempt to drive us from our strong citadels, to break our communities.

Though we did not give up the fight and our nation and the best of its pastors struggled desperately against a superior authority, the endless siege wore us out. There were traitors and weaklings, too. Many gave up or ran away. Part of our communities were dispersed, others died in the fighting.

Our Church disintegrated, in its structure, in its faith and in its moral perspective. Its institutions were interdicted, day by day they were cut off from the place where they drew their support – the living community. A significant part of its people became alienated from it, the youth slipped from its hands. The remains of the flock were divided by anxiety and fear, separated from their pastors. Despair conquered them.

'A time to tear down and a time to build', says the Preacher (Eccl. 3:3). There is a responsibility waiting for us and for our children – to rebuild the ruins, with the help of God, to resettle the Church, just as once the people of Israel did it, returning from captivity, so that the Church may serve us again as a 'powerful fortress against the enemy'. Although we were liberated from dictatorship, we live under constant threats and uncertainty of life. 'Our old enemy is discontented with us'.

2. We ask ourselves, in the words of Scripture, *'Brethren, what shall we do?'*

Firstly, 'Repent', as the Apostle Peter says (Acts 2: 38). Let us examine anew the basic issues of our lives, our presuppositions – 'our sins that bring death with them', suggests Sandor Makkai. Not just to identify external causes, but the inner ones as well – our spiritual and social sins. As a bishop of Transylvania once said, 'Let us rather be unfair and cruel with ourselves, than find external grounds to justify ourselves.' What is truly needed is a *general repentance* which will clear away our past guilt, and lift us up again as the first and necessary stage of our radical revival. By turning back to God, we can find ourselves again.

This is the spiritual and moral dimension to the answer to the question, 'What shall we do?', which seeks to identify the possibility of our going on and the conditions upon which our progress depends.

But the question demands an answer also on the concrete level of our religious life, the level of practical action and making plans. And the answers to the question in this respect may well constitute the subject of the bishop's speech according to traditional expectation. In other words: What programme do I propose to initiate, what do we want to see achieved in our Church?

And the following points will be important in the renewal of our religious life:

a) During recent times the Church lived from one

day to the next. Its activity was sporadic, it functioned properly only in some parts of the country and in other parts it died. At its worst, the deliberately destructive, oppressive mechanisms at the centre functioned well.

Against this, we must strive to develop what is universally needed: a conceptual church-politics that considers the Church *as a whole*. I am thinking of the organic unity of the earthly body of Christ and the strong relationship between the members and the body. And I am thinking of 'politics' in the noblest sense of the word: that activity which serves the common interests of the *polis*.

b) In this context what is absolutely necessary is an evaluation, carried out with mathematical precision, of the general situation of the Church and also the precise situation in this church district. This examination may well provide a starting point for other tasks to further the work of renewal. It can be carried out by research and by visiting the church districts and counties.

The task that is most urgent is to conduct a census of the present extent of the Church. We must find out our numbers and how many of us are left.

c) Though we are historically a Presbyterian Church, we have become too clerical. For centuries, in obvious and not-so-obvious ways, a struggle has continued in our Church between Presbyterianism and the role of the bishops. Yet we cannot separate ourselves from the full authority of the bishop. However, in the Communist period that role was overlaid with a monolithic centrism that recalled Caesarian-papism.

We must do away with this burdensome historical and Communist heritage. We must democratise and decentralise our religious institutions and liberate them from hierarchical, clerical and episcopal pressures. We must realise the autonomy of the church counties and congregations; we must affirm the right of self-government and administrative material independence. Church district unity must be realised by means of free association, together with a commitment to the universal public interest.

We must diminish, and accurately determine, the bishop's rights and sphere of authority. So for instance Church discipline and the synodical presidency must be made independent from the bishop.

d) In the light of the previous suggestions, the demand of the epoch and of the gospel is the realisation of a new *clerical code*, which gives value to the spirit of synodical-presbyterian heritage of our Church and goes beyond what has gone before on the road of evangelical evolution.

e) Our church district must review its social, clerical and international relationships, and must concentrate on developing a *new universal system of relationships*. Re-evaluation and renewal is necessary in the following respects:

– regarding the relation between the two Protestant Church districts, for unity;

– regarding relationships with all the Reformed Hungarian Churches, as a sign of unity, with special regard to the so-called minority churches (Czechoslovakia, the Soviet Union, Yugoslavia);

– regarding relationships with different Hungarian religious beliefs, for constructive measures of cooperation in certain areas as members of the Hungarian population (Roman Catholics, Baptists, Evangelicals);

– in the spirit of Christian unity with other Churches in the country (Orthodox, Greek Catholics);

– in the spirit of universal Christian unity with Churches from abroad and with international ecumenical organisations.

The opening up of these relationships and the changes taking place offer the promise of a *new ecumenical interrelationship*, free from protocol and formalism; a development that will be helped by the new possibilities and changed conditions of international and internal relations.

Practically, we must secure the complete overthrow of the one-sided State dependence which damaged the Church's most important interests and took away its freedom. We must establish a new kind of relationship between the State and the Church. The Church's autonomy must be reestablished. The chief principle must be that of 'a free church in a free state'. It is the only way to assure true freedom of religion.

f) Yet our Church must bind itself to society and to political life. It cannot exist above society. It cannot be marginalised. On the other hand, it cannot remain apolitical. The Church must share the social concerns of our country and its religious people.

It must have a definite point of view on political problems, contributing in its own way, with its own specific methodology and spirituality, to their solution. Thus its service of charity lightens suffering and poverty. The service of the Church also helps to heal the problems of the young and the aged. Rooted as it is in the life of our nation, our Church cannot be indifferent to questions of vital importance to the Hungarian minority.

g) In order to fulfil its social vocation and to be a 'strong fortress' to its people, our Church must avoid an exclusive and unsocial type of denominationalism and follow the tradition of the people's Church; it must realise that it needs all its people.

To that end it must undertake a strenuous mission work. It must create various forms of association and small church community structures, or at least reform the existing ones. The development of professional and well-planned work among our scattered minorities is a significant need, as is the foundation of new congregations made necessary by the social mobility of the past years.

This intensive missionary service necessitates the guaranteeing of an appropriate supply of pastors and the developing of new forms of service suitable for the needs thus identified.

h) It is a social service of the Church and the church building to restore denominational teaching which will be most effective and updated by using modern technical equipment and the press.

Church, education and the printing of books have been bound together in the service of our religious life since the Reformation.

The cause of the renewed Church may be served by the framework of a modern infrastructure, for example the use of audio-visual aids and up-to-date techniques, just as once the discovery of printing enabled the Reformation to spread.

i) The custodian and preserver of our cultural, historical and national values is our faith and Church. The State's Church-destroying policy, among others, focused these values and tried to suppress them.

For this reason, as part of our rebuilding we must pay great attention to our monuments, religious art and music, congregational traditions, graveyards and archives.

j) The development of financial and economic springs for the renewal demands a new assessment.

The most important part of the sustaining of the native Church in the future will be the voluntary donation given in Christian love. Donations from those with a living faith served in great manner to sustain schools in the past. Today additional material resources are needed; land, property, perhaps also the creation of financial reserves.

The introduction of a general sharing of taxation would mean a really new perspective and a new way of distributing financial resources in our economy. Our faith teaches, 'You ought to bear one another's burdens.' Only in this way can we support those congregations that are unable to support themselves; and in this way we can establish a really effective Church and evangelistic mission.

k) In the present miserable situation, when we must build up our Church almost from its ruins, the indispensable condition of renewal is foreign aid. There is no lack of active support and help from foreign Churches, Church organisations and faithful Christians. For this help not to melt away or be transformed into 'alms' to alleviate immediate needs, we must organise, direct and use it systematically. The organising of receiving and distributing the aid is as important as donation. Our Church must be wisely economical with foreign material resources and it must be geared to the right place and purpose.

Likewise we must reorganise the institution of

foreign study tours and scholarships, making good use of this help for the universal benefit of our impoverished Church, in spirituality and theology.

The future of our theological teaching and Church science depends in great measure upon the moral and material support of the foreign Churches and universities.

Last, but not least, I submit to the university of our Church two different proposals.

The first is identical with the so-called Appeal from Szilagycseh dated December 28th, 1989, in its eighth point, which reads as follows:

> The Native Church cannot live in the future for even a moment while the clergy bear in their conscience the burden of sins, injustices committed in the recent past. Those who were the suffering subjects of clerical injustice and episcopal dictatorship must be rehabilitated morally and also according to the law – legally. In the interest of achieving this, those involved should forward a complaint with authentic documentation to the respective disciplinary committees entrusted with the case. Congregations which were offended in their own right should proceed likewise. The need for a thorough knowledge of the situation necessitates that this too should be taken into account.

Because of the great number of cases involved, the rehabilitation and jurisdiction will introduce a new age in our Church. It is necessary that it should be done openly, and that it should be effective. This situation is like a dark period on the road to our Church's revival.

My second invitation is totally different. I propose: *let us build churches*.

Let us establish a national church-building material base. For almost fifty years the building of churches was prohibited. The people of our villages have moved *en masse* to the towns, have been settled in huge districts of apartment blocks where there are no churches. Our total congregation was growing, but the number of congregations and churches remained the same.

We must organise new congregations and build new churches. This is the task for our age and for our Church; it is a task like that of King Solomon in the Scriptures. As this service of installation proceeds, always before my eyes is the image of the example set by Domokos Szasz, Bishop of Transylvania in the last century, whose outstandingly important church-building activity preceded the general revival of the Transylvanian Church.

Let us do likewise as we move out of our prison, like those who built the wall against the destruction of Israel. The words of Nehemiah give us our trust:

> The work is extensive and spread out, and we are widely separated from each other along the wall. Wherever you hear the sound of the trumpet, join us there. Our God will fight for us' (Neh. 4: 19–20).

In our overwhelming work, God is leading us. Don't give up the fight! Let us build a Church, for his holy name; a shelter, a 'strong fortress' for the future.

Ilona Tokes was born on June 20th, 1990.

Readers in Britain who wish to make a financial contribution to the work of the Hungarian Reformed Diocese of Nagyvarad (Oradea) may send cheques (payable to Gezcy Istvan Ne.) to the following bank account:

Account B55174, Bank MNB 349-98007, OTP Debrecen, Debrecen, Hungary.

A list of projects and activities in which the Diocese is currently engaged may be obtained by writing to: The Secretary, Episcopia Reformata, 3700 Oradea, Str. Craiovei, 1, ROMANIA

Please enclose an international reply coupon.

The International Transylvanian Foundation

The Foundation was established in Budapest on May 29th 1990 by Laszlo Tokes, writer Andras Suto and company director Dezso Abraham. The following is taken from the Deed of Foundation:

'The Foundation aims to promote the remaining in Transylvania of the Hungarians living there, and the voluntary return to their Transylvanian homeland of those who have emigrated. The Foundation respects the sovereignty of Romania.

The Foundation identifies with the progressive

Transylvanian tolerance, ethnic and religious diversity, peaceful coexistence, and mutual understanding and appreciation. Transylvania is the common fatherland of Romanians, Hungarians, Germans, Jews, Saxons and other national minorities as well as various religions. In this spirit we support the homecoming not only of the Hungarians but also of the Romanians, the Germans, the Jews and every other nationality, as we hope that the afflicted can promote real reconciliation together.

The following help will be provided:

a) Assistance for homecoming or remaining;
b) Scholarships for further education in Romania;
c) Support of institutions of education and culture;
d) Support of church affairs;
e) Other support according to the instructions of the endower;
f) General support according to the resolution of the Board of Trustees;
g) Endowing and awarding a Foundation prize to honour activities . . . which are likely to help the Foundation achieve its aims.

Further information may be obtained from The International Transylvanian Foundation, H-1300 Budapest, PF.14. British readers wishing to contribute financially to the Foundation may make donations at any bank, quoting the following: sorting code 40 05 15, Midland Bank International Division, London; for the credit of the Hungarian Credit Bank, Account No. 35388403, reference International Transylvanian Foundation.

UNIVERSITY LIBRARY
NOTTINGHAM